A COMMUNICATIVE APPROACH TO
THE TOEIC® L&R TEST
Book 1: Elementary

Teruhiko Kadoyama
Simon Capper
Toshiaki Endo

JN061742

SEIBIDO

photographs by
iStockphoto

音声ファイルのダウンロード／ストリーミング

CD マーク表示がある箇所は、音声を弊社 HP より無料でダウンロード／ストリーミングすることができます。下記 URL の書籍詳細ページに音声ダウンロードアイコンがございますのでそちらから自習用音声としてご活用ください。

https://seibido.co.jp/ad645

A COMMUNICATIVE APPROACH TO THE TOEIC® L&R TEST
Book 1: Elementary

LINGUAPORTA

リンガポルタのご案内

> **リンガポルタ連動テキストをご購入の学生さんは、「リンガポルタ」を無料でご利用いただけます！**

　本テキストで学習していただく内容に準拠した問題を、オンライン学習システム「リンガポルタ」で学習していただくことができます。PCだけでなく、スマートフォンやタブレットでも学習できます。単語や文法、リスニング力などをよりしっかり身に付けていただくため、ぜひ積極的に活用してください。

　リンガポルタの利用にはアカウントとアクセスコードの登録が必要です。登録方法については下記ページにアクセスしてください。

https://www.seibido.co.jp/linguaporta/register.html

本テキスト「A COMMUNICATIVE APPROACH TO THE TOEIC® L&R TEST Book 1: Elementary」
のアクセスコードは下記です。

7252-2046-1231-0365-0003-0070-V7PB-P6EN

・リンガポルタの学習機能（画像はサンプルです。また、すべてのテキストに以下の4つの機能が用意されているわけではありません）

● 多肢選択

● 空所補充（音声を使っての聞き取り問題も可能）

● 単語並びかえ（マウスや手で単語を移動）

● マッチング（マウスや手で単語を移動）

は し が き

　本書は、A COMMUNICATIVE APPROACH TO THE TOEIC® L&R TEST シリーズの初級編であり、主に TOEIC® Listening and Reading Test（以下、TOEIC L&R テスト）を初めて受験する方を対象としています。TOEIC L&R テスト対策のテキストは数多く出版されていますが、本書の特徴は、タイトルが示すように、コミュニケーションに焦点を当てたアプローチを採用した試験対策テキストであるという点です。具体的には、実践形式で練習問題を解いた後、問題で使われた対話や文書を活用して、パートナーと互いに英語で質問したり、質問に答えたりするコミュニケーション演習が本書には豊富に含まれています。試験対策の授業では予想問題を解くのが中心で、英語を話す機会がほとんどない場合もありますが、このテキストで学習することにより、単に TOEIC L&R テストのスコアアップだけではなく、英語のコミュニケーション能力を向上させることも可能となるでしょう。

　この他にも本書には次のような特徴があります。

　まず、各ユニットの最初にある Vocabulary のセクションでは、語彙の中でも特に派生語の増強に焦点を当てています。Part 5 の文法問題では正しい品詞を選ぶ問題が数多く出題されますが、派生語の知識を増やすことで、未知の単語であっても、語尾から意味や品詞を推測できるようになるでしょう。

　次に、各パートの問題を解くうえで知っておくべき重要項目を「解法のコツ」としてまとめており、効率的な学習が可能です。Part 3〜4 の図表問題や Part 6 の文挿入問題など、TOEIC L&R テストには特徴的な設問がいろいろありますが、解法のコツをマスターすることでそれらにも十分対応できるはずです。

　この他にも、本書は Web 英語学習システムの LINGUAPORTA（リンガポルタ）に対応していますので、パソコンやスマートフォンを使ったモバイル・ラーニングが可能です。

　TOEIC L&R テストは約 2 時間で 200 問の問題を解かなければならず、スコアアップを図るにはやはり地道な英語学習が必要とされます。本書での学習が、皆さんの目標スコア獲得や英語コミュニケーション能力の涵養に役立てば、筆者としてこれ以上の喜びはありません。

　また、本書の刊行にあたっては、成美堂の佐野英一郎社長、そして編集部の工藤隆志氏、萩原美奈子氏に多大なご尽力を賜りました。衷心よりお礼申し上げます。

角山照彦
Simon Capper
遠藤利昌

Table of Contents

本 書 の 構 成 と 使 い 方

　本書は、オフィス、ショッピング、レストランなど、TOEIC L&R テストに頻出のテーマを取り上げた全 14 ユニットで構成されています。また、各ユニットは次のような構成になっています。

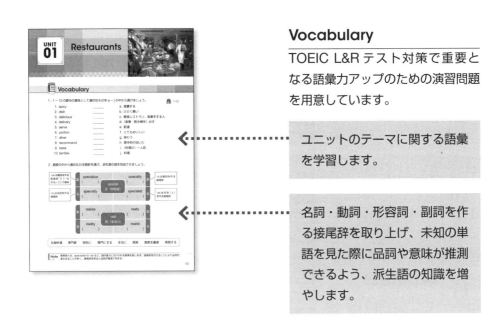

Vocabulary

TOEIC L&R テスト対策で重要となる語彙力アップのための演習問題を用意しています。

> ユニットのテーマに関する語彙を学習します。

> 名詞・動詞・形容詞・副詞を作る接尾辞を取り上げ、未知の単語を見た際に品詞や意味が推測できるよう、派生語の知識を増やします。

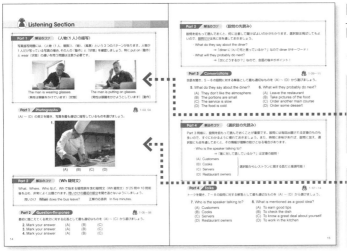

Listening Section

Part 1～4 について、解法のコツと演習問題を用意しています。

> 頻出問題の解き方など、各パートの問題を解く際に必要な解法のコツを学習します。

> 解法のコツ で取り上げた内容を含む演習問題に取り組むことで実践力アップを目指します。

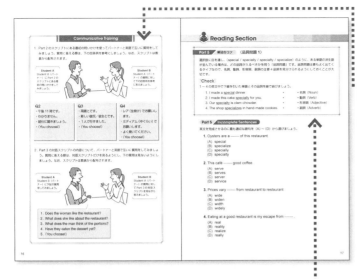

Communicative Training (Listening Section)

Part 2～4 で取り上げた応答や対話・トークを使ってパートナーと互いに英語で質問をしたり、質問に答えたりする演習です。

Reading Section

Part 5～7 について、解法のコツと演習問題を用意しています。

頻出問題の解き方など、各パートの問題を解く際に必要な解法のコツを学習します。

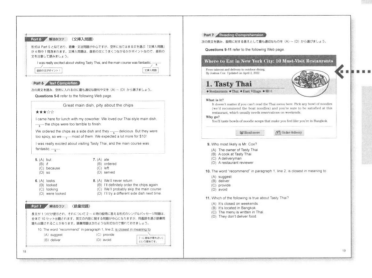

解法のコツ で取り上げた内容を含む演習問題に取り組むことで実践力アップを目指します。

Communicative Training (Reading Section)

Part 7 で取り上げた文書を使ってパートナーと互いに英語で質問をしたり、質問に答えたりする演習です。

TOEIC® Listening and Reading Test について

　TOEIC® Listening and Reading Test（以下、TOEIC L&R テスト）は、アメリカの非営利団体 Educational Testing Service（ETS）によって開発されたテストです。TOEIC とは、**T**est **O**f **E**nglish for **I**nternational **C**ommunication の略称で、オフィスや日常生活における英語コミュニケーション能力を幅広く測定するテストですが、TOEIC L&R テストは、その中でも特に Listening と Reading の能力を測定するものです。（TOEIC テストには、TOEIC L&R テストの他にも TOEIC® Speaking & Writing Tests や TOEIC® Speaking Test があります。）

評価方法

　TOEIC L&R テストの結果は、合格や不合格ではなく、10 点から 990 点までのスコアで評価されます（リスニングセクション：5〜495 点、リーディングセクション：5〜495 点）。トータルスコアの基準は常に一定であり、英語能力に変化がない限りスコアも一定に保たれます。

問題形式

　リスニングセクション（約 45 分間・100問）とリーディングセクション（75 分間・100問）から構成されおり、約 2 時間で 200問の問題に解答しなければなりません。各セクションは、次の表が示すように、7 つのパートに分かれています。

セクション	パート	名称		形式	問題数
リスニングセクション	1	Photographs	写真描写問題	4 択	6 問
	2	Question-Response	応答問題	3 択	25 問
	3	Conversations	会話問題	4 択	39 問
	4	Talks	説明文問題	4 択	30 問
リーディングセクション	5	Incomplete Sentences	短文穴埋め問題	4 択	30 問
	6	Text Completion	長文穴埋め問題	4 択	16 問
	7	Reading Comprehension	読解問題	4 択	54 問

また、各パートの形式は以下のとおりです。

Part 1　Photographs

　1枚の写真について4つの短い説明文が1度だけ放送され、4つのうち写真を最も適切に描写しているものを選ぶ問題です。問題用紙には右のような写真のみで、説明文は印刷されていません。実際のテストでは6問出題され、解答時間は1問あたり約5秒です。

【問題例】
1.

Part 2　Question-Response

　1つの質問（または発言）と、3つの応答がそれぞれ1度だけ放送され、質問に対して最も適切な応答を3つの中から選ぶ問題です。問題用紙には質問も応答も印刷されていません。実際のテストでは25問出題され、解答時間は1問あたり約5秒です。

【問題例】
7. Mark your answer on your answer sheet.

Part 3　Conversations

　会話が1度だけ放送され、その後に設問が続きます。会話は印刷されていません。問題用紙の設問と4つの選択肢を読み、その中から最も適切なものを選ぶ問題です。実際のテストでは39問出題されます。解答時間は1問あたり約8秒ですが、図表問題のみ約12秒となっています。

【問題例】
32. Where does the woman work?

(A) At a restaurant
(B) At a hospital
(C) At a school
(D) At a post office

Part 4　Talks

　アナウンスや電話のメッセージなどの説明文が1度だけ放送され、その後に設問が続きます。説明文は印刷されていません。問題用紙の設問と4つの選択肢を読み、その中から最も適切なものを選ぶ問題です。実際のテストでは30問出題されます。解答時間は1問あたり約8秒ですが、図表問題のみ約12秒となっています。

【問題例】
71. What is being advertised?

(A) A pharmacy
(B) A movie theater
(C) A fitness center
(D) A supermarket

Part 5 Incomplete Sentences

4 つの選択肢の中から最も適切なものを選び、不完全な文を完成させる問題です。実際のテストでは 30 問出題されます。

【問題例】

101. Oysters are a ------- of this restaurant.

    (A) special
    (B) specialize
    (C) specially
    (D) specialty

Part 6 Text Completion

4 つの選択肢の中から最も適切なものを選び、不完全な文書を完成させる問題です。実際のテストでは、1 つの長文に対して 4 問ずつ問題があり、合計 16 問出題されます。

【問題例】

Online shopping is a fast-growing market in the U.S. In a survey ------- 131. in May last year, 40 percent of U.S.-based Internet users answered that they bought goods online several times a month.

131.(A) conduct
    (B) conducting
    (C) conducted
    (D) conducts

Part 7 Reading Comprehension

様々な形式の文書が提示され、それに関する設問と 4 つの選択肢を読んでその中から最も適切なものを選ぶ問題です。実際のテストでは、1 つの文書に関する問題（シングルパッセージ問題）が 29 問、複数の文書に関する問題（ダブルパッセージ問題・トリプルパッセージ問題）が 25 問出題されます。

【問題例】

Dear all,
I hope this e-mail finds you all well.

147. The word "recommend" in paragraph 1, line 7, is closest in meaning to

    (A) suggest
    (B) deliver
    (C) provide
    (D) avoid

UNIT 01 Restaurants

 ## Vocabulary

1. 1 ～ 10 の語句の意味として適切なものを a ～ j の中から選びましょう。　　🎧 1-02

1. spicy	＿＿＿＿		a. 推薦する
2. dish	＿＿＿＿		b. ひどく悪い
3. delicious	＿＿＿＿		c. 軽食レストラン、食事をする人
4. delivery	＿＿＿＿		d.（食事・飲み物を）出す
5. serve	＿＿＿＿		e. 配達
6. portion	＿＿＿＿		f. とてもおいしい
7. diner	＿＿＿＿		g. 味わう
8. recommend	＿＿＿＿		h. 香辛料の効いた
9. taste	＿＿＿＿		i.（料理の）一人前
10. terrible	＿＿＿＿		j. 料理

2. 語群の中から適切な日本語訳を選び、派生語の図を完成させましょう。

-ize は動詞を作る接尾辞*で「～化する」という意味

-ty は名詞を作る接尾辞

| 動 | specialize （　　　） |
| 名 | specialty （　　　） |

special
形（特別な）

| specially （　　　） | 副 |
| specialist （　　　） | 名 |

-ly は副詞を作る接尾辞

-ist は名詞（人）を作る接尾辞

| 動 | realize （　　　） |
| 名 | reality （　　　） |

real
形（本当の）

| really （　　　） | 副 |
| realist （　　　） | 名 |

┌───┐
　名物料理　　専門家　　特別に　　専門にする　　本当に　　現実　　現実主義者　　実現する
└───┘

Note 接尾辞とは、specialist の -ist など、語の後ろに付けられる要素を指します。接尾辞を付けることにより品詞が変化することが多く、接尾辞を見ると品詞が推測できます。

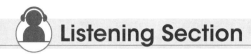 **Listening Section**

Part 1 解法のコツ 〈人物（1人）の描写〉

写真描写問題には、〈人物（1人、複数）〉、〈物〉、〈風景〉という3つのパターンがあります。人物が1人だけ写っている写真の場合、その人の「動作」と「状態」を確認しましょう。特に put on（動作）と wear（状態）の違いを問う問題は注意が必要です。

The man is wearing glasses.
（男性は眼鏡をかけています）［状態］

The man is putting on glasses.
（男性は眼鏡をかけようとしています）［動作］

Part 1 Photographs   1-03, 04

（A）〜（D）の英文を聞き、写真を最も適切に描写しているものを選びましょう。

1.

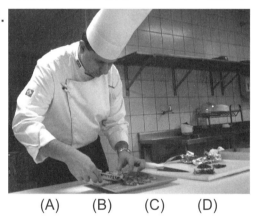

(A)   (B)   (C)   (D)

Part 2 解法のコツ 〈Wh 疑問文〉

What、Where、Who など、Wh で始まる疑問詞を含む疑問文（Wh 疑問文）が 25 問中 10 問前後を占め、非常によく出題されます。問いかけの最初の部分を聞き逃さないようにしましょう。

問いかけ When does the bus leave?   正解の応答例 In five minutes.

Part 2 Question-Response   1-05〜08

最初に聞こえてくる英文に対する応答として最も適切なものを（A）〜（C）から選びましょう。

2. Mark your answer.   (A)   (B)   (C)
3. Mark your answer.   (A)   (B)   (C)
4. Mark your answer.   (A)   (B)   (C)

Part 3 解法のコツ 〈設問の先読み〉

設問を前もって読んでおくと、何に注意して聞けばよいのかがわかります。選択肢は飛ばしてもよいので、設問だけは先に目を通しておきましょう。

・What do they say about the diner?

　　　⇒「diner について何と言っているか？」なので diner がキーワード！

・What will they probably do next?

　　　⇒「次にどうするか？」なので、会話の後半がポイント！

Part 3 **Conversations** 1-09〜11

会話を聞き、5〜6の設問に対する解答として最も適切なものを（A）〜（D）から選びましょう。

5. What do they say about the diner?

　(A) They don't like the atmosphere.
　(B) The portions are small.
　(C) The service is slow.
　(D) The food is cold.

6. What will they probably do next?

　(A) Leave the restaurant
　(B) Take pictures of the food
　(C) Order another main course
　(D) Order some dessert

Part 4 解法のコツ 〈選択肢の先読み〉

Part 3 同様に、設問を前もって読んでおくことが重要です。設問には毎回出題される定番のものも多いので、すぐにわかるように慣れておきましょう。また、時間に余裕があれば、設問に加え、選択肢にも目を通しておくと、その情報が理解の助けとなる場合があります。

・Who is the speaker talking to?

　　　⇒「誰に対して話しているか？」は定番の設問！

　(A) Customers
　(B) Cooks
　(C) Servers
　(D) Restaurant owners

選択肢からレストランに関する話だと推測可能！

Part 4 **Talks** 1-12〜14

トークを聞き、7〜8の設問に対する解答として最も適切なものを（A）〜（D）から選びましょう。

7. Who is the speaker talking to?

　(A) Customers
　(B) Cooks
　(C) Servers
　(D) Restaurant owners

8. What is mentioned as a good idea?

　(A) To earn good tips
　(B) To check the dish
　(C) To know a great deal about yourself
　(D) To work in the kitchen

1. Part 2 のスクリプトにある最初の問いかけを使ってパートナーと英語で互いに質問をして
みましょう。質問に答える際は、下の回答例を参考にしましょう。なお、スクリプトは教
員から配布されます。

Student A
Student B（パート
ナー）に Part 2 の
スクリプトにある最
初の問いかけをして
みましょう。

Student B
Student A（パート
ナー）の質問に対し
て下の回答例を参考
に答えましょう。

Q2
・午後 11 時です。
・わかりません。
・給仕に聞きましょう。
・(You choose!)

Q3
・両親とです。
・新しい彼氏／彼女とです。
・1 人で行きました。
・(You choose!)

Q4
・レア（生焼け）でお願いし
ます。
・ミディアム（中ぐらい）で
お願いします。
・よく焼いてください。
・(You choose!)

2. Part 3 の対話スクリプトの内容について、パートナーと英語で互いに質問をしてみましょ
う。質問に答える際は、対話スクリプトだけを見るようにし、下の質問は見ないようにし
ましょう。なお、スクリプトは教員から配布されます。

Student A
Student B（パート
ナー）に下記の質問
をしてみましょう。

Student B
Student A（パート
ナー）の質問に対し
て Part 3 の対話ス
クリプトを見ながら
答えましょう。

1. Does the woman like the restaurant?
2. What does she like about the restaurant?
3. What does the man think of the portions?
4. Have they eaten the dessert yet?
5. (You choose!)

Reading Section

Part 5 / 解法のコツ 〈品詞問題 1〉

選択肢に目を通し、（special / specially / specialty / specialize）のように、ある単語の派生語が並んでいる場合は、どの品詞が入るべきかを問う「品詞問題」です。品詞問題は最もよく出てくるタイプなので、名詞、動詞、形容詞、副詞の主要 4 品詞を見分けられるようにしておくことが大切です。

Check

1 ～ 4 の英文中で下線を引いた単語とその品詞を線で結びましょう。

1. I made a <u>special</u> dinner.   •   • 名詞（Noun）
2. I made this cake <u>specially</u> for you.   •   • 動詞（Verb）
3. Our <u>specialty</u> is clam chowder.   •   • 形容詞（Adjective）
4. The shop <u>specializes</u> in hand-made cookies. •   • 副詞（Adverb）

Part 5 / Incomplete Sentences

英文を完成させるのに最も適切な語句を（A）～（D）から選びましょう。

1. Oysters are a ------- of this restaurant.

  (A) special
  (B) specialize
  (C) specially
  (D) specialty

2. This café ------- good coffee.

  (A) serve
  (B) serves
  (C) server
  (D) service

3. Prices vary ------- from restaurant to restaurant.

  (A) wide
  (B) widen
  (C) width
  (D) widely

4. Eating at a good restaurant is my escape from ------- .

  (A) real
  (B) reality
  (C) realize
  (D) really

形式は Part 5 と似ており、語彙・文法問題が中心ですが、空所に当てはまる文を選ぶ「文挿入問題」が 4 問中 1 問含まれます。文挿入問題は、直前の文にうまくつながるかがポイントなので、直前の文を注意して読みましょう。

I was really excited about visiting Tasty Thai, and the main course was fantastic. -------- .
8.

直前の文がポイント！

文挿入問題

Part 6 / **Text Completion**

次の英文を読み、空所に入れるのに最も適切な語句や文を（A）～（D）から選びましょう。

Questions 5-8 refer to the following Web page.

Great main dish, pity about the chips

★★★☆☆

I came here for lunch with my coworker. We loved our Thai-style main dish, -------- the chips were too terrible to finish.
5.

We ordered the chips as a side dish and they -------- delicious. But they were
6.
too spicy, so we -------- most of them. We expected a lot more for $10!
7.

I was really excited about visiting Tasty Thai, and the main course was
fantastic. -------- .
8.

---

5. (A) but
(B) if
(C) because
(D) so

6. (A) looks
(B) looked
(C) looking
(D) were looked

7. (A) ate
(B) ordered
(C) left
(D) served

8. (A) We'll never return.
(B) I'll definitely order the chips again.
(C) We'll probably skip the main course.
(D) I'll try a different side dish next time.

長文が 1 つだけ提示され、それについて 2 ～ 4 問の設問に答える形式のシングルパッセージ問題は、全体で 10 セット出題されます。英文の内容に関する問題が中心になりますが、同義語を選ぶ語彙問題も出題されることがあります。語彙問題は次のような形式なので慣れておきましょう。

10. The word "recommend" in paragraph 1, line 2, is closest in meaning to

(A) suggest
(C) provide

(B) deliver
(D) avoid

「～に意味が最も近い」
という意味です。

次の英文を読み、設問に対する答えとして最も適切なものを（A）〜（D）から選びましょう。

Questions 9-11 refer to the following Web page.

Where to Eat in New York City: 10 Must-Visit Restaurants

From takeout and delivery to outdoor dining.
By Joshua Cox Updated on April 2, 2022

1. Tasty Thai

◆ Restaurants ◆ Thai ◆ East Village ◆ $$$$

What is it?
   It doesn't matter if you can't read the Thai menu here. Pick any bowl of noodles (we'd recommend the boat noodles) and you're sure to be satisfied at this restaurant, which usually needs reservations on weekends.
Why go?
   You'll taste bowls of noodle soups that make you feel like you're in Bangkok.

 Read more 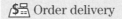 Order delivery

9. Who most likely is Mr. Cox?

(A) The owner of Tasty Thai
(B) A cook at Tasty Thai
(C) A deliveryman
(D) A restaurant reviewer

10. The word "recommend" in paragraph 1, line 2, is closest in meaning to

(A) suggest
(B) deliver
(C) provide
(D) avoid

11. Which of the following is true about Tasty Thai?

(A) It's closed on weekends.
(B) It's located in Bangkok.
(C) The menu is written in Thai.
(D) They don't deliver food.

Communicative Training

Part 7 で取り上げたウェブページを使ってパートナーと英語で互いに質問をしてみましょう。答える際は、"Yes." や "No." だけで終わらないよう適宜、情報を追加しましょう。

Student A
Student B（パートナー）に下記の質問をしてみましょう。

Student B
Student A（パートナー）の質問に対して Part 7 の英文を見ながら答えましょう。

1. Who wrote the review?

2. When was the review updated?

3. What is the name of the restaurant?

4. What dish does the reviewer recommend?

5. Is the restaurant in Bangkok?

6. Does the restaurant deliver food?

7. (You choose!)

UNIT 02 Offices

Vocabulary

1. 1 〜 10 の語句の意味として適切なものを a 〜 j の中から選びましょう。　🎧 1-15

1. reply	＿＿＿＿	a. 詳細
2. document	＿＿＿＿	b. 配布資料
3. confirm	＿＿＿＿	c. 便利な、都合が良い
4. in advance	＿＿＿＿	d. 文書
5. convenient	＿＿＿＿	e. 〜の予定を変更する
6. attend	＿＿＿＿	f. 確認する
7. reschedule	＿＿＿＿	g. 〜を参照する
8. refer to	＿＿＿＿	h. 返事をする
9. detail	＿＿＿＿	i. 前もって
10. handout	＿＿＿＿	j. 出席する

2. 語群の中から適切な日本語訳を選び、派生語の図を完成させましょう。

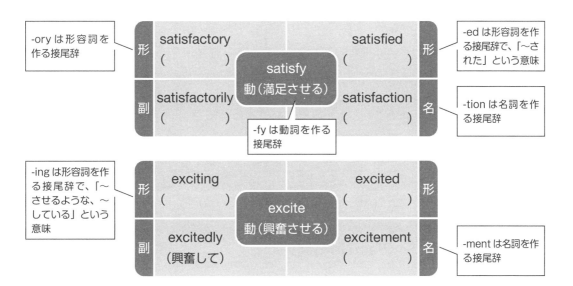

-ory は形容詞を作る接尾辞				
形	satisfactory（　　　）		satisfied（　　　）	形 -ed は形容詞を作る接尾辞で、「〜された」という意味
		satisfy 動（満足させる）		
副	satisfactorily（　　　）		satisfaction（　　　）	名 -tion は名詞を作る接尾辞

-fy は動詞を作る接尾辞

-ing は形容詞を作る接尾辞で、「〜させるような、〜している」という意味				
形	exciting（　　　）		excited（　　　）	形
		excite 動（興奮させる）		
副	excitedly（興奮して）		excitement（　　　）	名 -ment は名詞を作る接尾辞

満足のいくように　満足できる　満足した　満足　興奮させるような　興奮　興奮した

21

Listening Section

Part 1 　解法のコツ　　〈物の位置〉

〈人物（1人、複数）〉、〈物〉、〈風景〉という3つのパターンのうち、〈物〉が中心の写真の場合には、その「位置」と「状態」を確認しましょう。位置関係は、前置詞がポイントになります。

⟩Check⟨

枠の中から適切な前置詞を選び、1～4の英文を完成させましょう。

1. A is (　　　　　) the table.
2. B is (　　　　　) the table.
3. C is (　　　　　) the chair.
4. D is (　　　　　) the table.

above　　behind　　beside　　between　　on　　under

Part 1 　**Photographs**　　　　　　　　　　　　　🎧 1-16, 17

(A) ～ (D) の英文を聞き、写真を最も適切に描写しているものを選びましょう。

1.

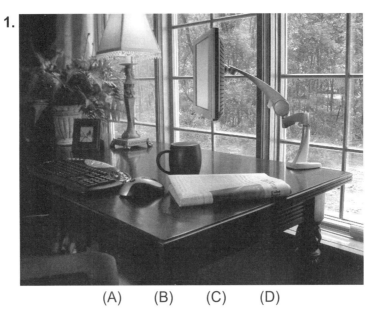

(A)　　　(B)　　　(C)　　　(D)

Part 2 　解法のコツ　　〈**Yes/No 疑問文**〉

Yes か No で答えることが可能な疑問文（Yes/No 疑問文）も Wh 疑問文と並んでよく出題されます。「よくわかりません」のように、応答は必ずしも Yes/No で始まるとは限らないので注意しましょう。

　問いかけ　　　Has everyone shown up for the meeting yet?
　正解の応答例　Sorry. I have no idea.

最初に聞こえてくる英文に対する応答として最も適切なものを（A）〜（C）から選びましょう。

2. Mark your answer.　　(A)　　　(B)　　　(C)
3. Mark your answer.　　(A)　　　(B)　　　(C)
4. Mark your answer.　　(A)　　　(B)　　　(C)

Part 3 / 解法のコツ　〈定番の設問〉

会話の話題や場所、話し手の職業など、毎回出題される定番の設問があるので、設問を見たらすぐにわかるように慣れておきましょう。

> most likely で「おそらく」という意味

・What are the speakers discussing?　　　⇒会話の話題がポイント！
・Where <u>most likely</u> are the speakers?　　⇒会話が行われている場所がポイント！
・Where do the speakers <u>most likely</u> work?　⇒話し手の職業・職場がポイント！
・What does the man suggest the woman do?　⇒男性が女性に提案している内容がポイント！

Part 3 **Conversations** 1-22〜24

会話を聞き、5〜7の設問に対する解答として最も適切なものを（A）〜（D）から選びましょう。

5. What are the speakers discussing?

(A) The woman's trip
(B) The man's schedule
(C) Their health
(D) Emma's injury

6. Where will the man most likely go tomorrow?

(A) To the airport
(B) To Emma's house
(C) To the woman's office
(D) To the hospital

7. What does the woman suggest?

(A) They should meet on Friday.
(B) They should go to the hospital.
(C) The man should cancel his appointment.
(D) She should have a medical checkup.

Part 4 / 解法のコツ 〈Talk の種類〉

1人の話し手によるトークには、電話のメッセージやラジオ放送、店内放送など、様々な種類が登場します。実際の問題ではトークが始まる前に次のような指示文が読まれるので、そこでトークの種類がわかります。トークの種類によって内容をある程度推測できるので、慣れておきましょう。

> トークの種類が示されます。

Questions 71-73 refer to the following telephone message.

> 「〜に関するものだ」という意味です。

⟩Check⟨

1 〜 5 の英文中で下線を引いた語句とその日本語訳を線で結びましょう。

1. Questions XXX-XXX refer to the following introduction. ・ ・講習会の抜粋
2. Questions XXX-XXX refer to the following excerpt from a meeting. ・ ・放送
3. Questions XXX-XXX refer to the following broadcast. ・ ・会議の抜粋
4. Questions XXX-XXX refer to the following excerpt from a workshop. ・ ・お知らせ
5. Questions XXX-XXX refer to the following announcement. ・ ・紹介

Part 4 / Talks

 1-25〜27

トークを聞き、8 〜 10 の設問に対する解答として最も適切なものを（A）〜（D）から選びましょう。

8. Who is Jeffrey Thomas?

(A) An athlete
(B) A newspaper reporter
(C) A sports announcer
(D) An assistant

9. When will Jeffrey Thomas return to the office?

(A) In an hour
(B) May 1
(C) May 3
(D) May 10

10. What should you do if you want to leave a message?

(A) Press 1
(B) Press 3
(C) Wait for the sound of the beep
(D) Call his assistant

1. Part 2 のスクリプトにある最初の問いかけを使ってパートナーと英語で互いに質問をして
   みましょう。質問に答える際は、下の回答例を参考にしましょう。なお、スクリプトは教
   員から配布されます。

Student A
Student B（パート
ナー）に Part 2 の
スクリプトにある最
初の問いかけをして
みましょう。

Student B
Student A（パート
ナー）の質問に対し
て下の回答例を参考
に答えましょう。

Q2	Q3	Q4
・はい、毎月出張に出かけます。 ・いいえ、年に1回だけです。 ・いいえ、年に数回だけです。 ・（You choose!）	・ええ、（それらは）私のです。ありがとうございます。 ・いいえ、（それらは）私のではありません。 ・いいえ、（それらは）彼のです。 ・（You choose!）	・ええ、とても忙しいです。 ・ええ、この仕事を終わらせなければなりません。 ・いいえ、ただ e メールを確認しているだけです。 ・（You choose!）

2. Part 4 のスクリプトの内容について、パートナーと英語で互いに質問をしてみましょう。
   質問に答える際は、スクリプトだけを見るようにし、下の質問は見ないようにしましょう。
   なお、スクリプトは教員から配布されます。

Student A
Student B（パート
ナー）に下記の質問
をしてみましょう。

Student B
Student A（パート
ナー）の質問に対し
て Part 4 のスクリ
プトを見ながら答え
ましょう。

1. Who recorded the message?
2. Who is Jeffrey Thomas?
3. Who does he work for?
4. When will he be back in the office?
5. (You choose!)

Reading Section

品詞問題で問われる品詞は、主に名詞、動詞、形容詞、副詞の 4 つです。形容詞と副詞は共に「説明を加える」役割を果たすため区別が難しいですが、確実に見分けられるようにしましょう。

形容詞	<u>名詞</u>に説明を加えます。
副　詞	名詞以外（動詞、形容詞、副詞など）に説明を加えます。

Check

網掛けの語に注意して 1 ～ 4 の英文中のカッコ内から正しい語を選び○で囲みましょう。

1. We'll open a （new / newly） office in New York.
2. Betty opened the box （excited / excitedly）.
3. The results were （satisfactory / satisfactorily）.
4. This software is （wonderful / wonderfully） easy to use.

Part 5 Incomplete Sentences

英文を完成させるのに最も適切な語句を（A）～（D）から選びましょう。

1. Fill out this form ------- and send it back to me.

(A) complete
(B) completely
(C) completion
(D) completed

2. Make sure you bring the ------- documents with you.

(A) necessarily
(B) necessity
(C) necessitate
(D) necessary

3. They looked ------- to see the president standing by the front door.

(A) surprised
(B) surprise
(C) surprising
(D) surprisingly

4. Ms. White has done a very ------- job.

(A) satisfy
(B) satisfaction
(C) satisfactory
(D) satisfactorily

Part 6 では、手紙や e メール、メモ、広告、通知、指示など、様々な種類の文書が登場します。文書の種類によって書式上の特徴があるので、文書の種類を即座に掴むことが重要です。また、実際の問題では次のような指示文が記載されるので、そこで文書の種類がわかります。

Questions 131-134 refer to the following <u>Web page</u>.

文書の種類が示されます。

☀Check☀

1 〜 5 の英文中で下線を引いた単語とその日本語訳を線で結びましょう。

1. Questions XXX-XXX refer to the following <u>advertisement</u>. •　　•記事
2. Questions XXX-XXX refer to the following <u>policy</u>. •　　•通知
3. Questions XXX-XXX refer to the following <u>article</u>. •　　•方針
4. Questions XXX-XXX refer to the following <u>notice</u>. •　　•指示
5. Questions XXX-XXX refer to the following <u>instructions</u>. •　　•広告

Part 6　Text Completion

次の英文を読み、空所に入れるのに最も適切な語句や文を（A）〜（D）から選びましょう。

Questions 5-8 refer to the following memo.

Dear Glenn,

------- you were out, Ms. Claire Higgins from Globe Media called about your
5.
meeting with her next Monday. She asked me to tell you that she is unable to
meet you on that day, so she would like to ------- to Tuesday at 10 A.M. Could
6.
you contact her to confirm if the new date and time is convenient for you? For
your information, she can be contacted at 03-1234-5678 and ------- in her
7.
office all afternoon.

------- .
8.

Best regards,
Helen

---

5. (A) Though
(B) Unless
(C) While
(D) Since

6. (A) cancel
(B) reschedule
(C) attend
(D) reserve

7. (A) was
(B) has been
(C) are
(D) will be

8. (A) Thank you in advance.
(B) I hope you are well.
(C) That was very kind of you.
(D) Sorry for the sudden change.

Part 7 で出題される文書の中でも eメールは文書形式の 1 つです。次の書式例で書式の特徴に慣れておきましょう。

eメールの書式例

From:
To:
Date:
Subject:
Attachment:

■ヘッダー
送信者、受信者、日付、件名、添付物が記されます。件名(Subject)は概要理解のヒントになるので必ず確認しましょう。

Dear Mr. Smith,

■本文
最初に、宛先（＝受信者）が記されます。Dear Mr. Smith のように、Dear から始まることが多いですが、親しい間柄の場合、Hi, Rick のようになることもあります。
次に、用件が述べられ、ここが問題の中心になるので、じっくり読みましょう。結びは、(Yours) Sincerely のほか、(Best) Regards などもよく使われます。

Sincerely,

John Wilson
Hiring Manager
ABC Bank

■フッター
送信者の氏名、所属（役職、部署、会社名）が記されます。

採用担当マネージャーという意味です。

次の英文を読み、設問に対する答えとして最も適切なものを（A）～（D）から選びましょう。

Questions 9-12 refer to the following e-mail.

To:	allstaff@creativecommunications.com
From:	j.turner@creativecommunications.com
Date:	June 16
Subject:	Mr. Morales' welcome party

Dear all,

I hope this e-mail finds you all well. I'm mailing to invite you to Mr. Martin Morales' welcome party.

As you know, Mr. Morales joined the customer service team last week, so we are planning to go out for dinner this Friday to welcome him to the team. I'd be happy if you could join us. Please refer to the details below:

Date: Friday, June 20
Location: Taylor's Steakhouse
Time: 7 P.M. – 9 P.M.

Please confirm if you can attend by tomorrow.
I'm looking forward to seeing you all there.

Best regards,
Josh

9. What is the purpose of the e-mail?

(A) To reply to an invitation
(B) To ask for suggestions for a party
(C) To extend an invitation
(D) To invite Mr. Morales to a party

10. What is true about Mr. Morales?

(A) He is the host of the party.
(B) He is a member of the customer service team.
(C) He joined the customer service team on June 16.
(D) He left the customer service team last week.

11. The word "confirm" in paragraph 4, line 1, is closest in meaning to

(A) extend
(B) inform
(C) receive
(D) decline

12. What is the receiver of the e-mail asked to do?

(A) To volunteer for an event
(B) To invite Mr. Morales
(C) To suggest a new plan
(D) To reply to Josh

Communicative Training

Part 7 で取り上げた e メールを使ってパートナーと英語で互いに質問をしてみましょう。答える際は、"Yes." や "No." だけで終わらないよう適宜、情報を追加しましょう。

Student A
Student B（パートナー）に下記の質問をしてみましょう。

Student B
Student A（パートナー）の質問に対して Part 7 の英文を見ながら答えましょう。

1. When was this e-mail sent?
2. Who wrote this e-mail?
3. Who is Mr. Morales?
4. When will the party be held?
5. What day of the week will the party be held?
6. Where will the party take place?
7. (You choose!)

UNIT 03 Daily Life

 Vocabulary

1. 1～10の語句の意味として適切なものをa～jの中から選びましょう。 1-28

1. direction	_____	a. 正式な
2. field trip	_____	b. 専門家
3. profession	_____	c. 遠足、校外学習
4. psychology	_____	d. 調査
5. industry	_____	e. 職業
6. formal	_____	f.（人）を車で拾う
7. survey	_____	g. 方向
8. massive	_____	h. 大量の
9. pick up	_____	i. 心理学
10. expert	_____	j. 産業

2. 語群の中から適切な日本語訳を選び、派生語の図を完成させましょう。

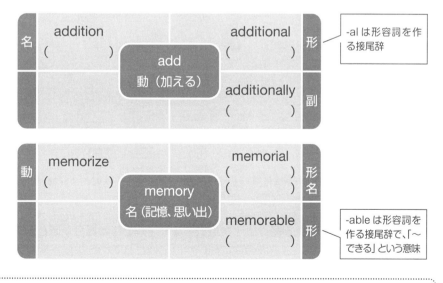

名 addition （　　　　）
形 additional （　　　　）　-al は形容詞を作る接尾辞
add 動（加える）
副 additionally （　　　　）

動 memorize （　　　　）
形 memorial （　　　　）
名 memory 名（記憶、思い出）
形 memorable （　　　　）　-able は形容詞を作る接尾辞で、「～できる」という意味

> 追加の　　追加　　その上、さらに　　記念の　　忘れられない　　記念碑　　暗記する

Listening Section

Part 1 解法のコツ 〈人物（2人）の描写〉

2人の人物が写っている写真の場合、「向かい合っている」や「並んでいる」のように、位置関係を確認しましょう。

They are facing each other.

（彼らは向かい合っています）

They are standing side by side.

（彼らは並んで立っています）

Part 1 Photographs 🎧 1-29, 30

（A）〜（D）の英文を聞き、写真を最も適切に描写しているものを選びましょう。

1.

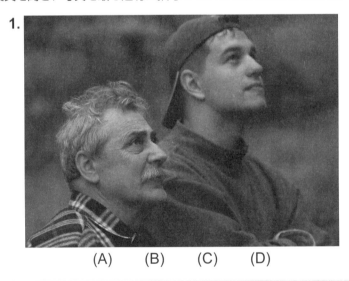

(A)　　(B)　　(C)　　(D)

Part 2 解法のコツ 〈同一単語の繰り返し 1〉

最初の問いかけに出てきた単語が入った選択肢は不正解である場合がほとんどです。問いかけが理解できなかった受験者は、選択肢の中に問いかけに使われていた単語が聞こえるとついその選択肢を選ぶ傾向があるため、出題者は意図的に不正解の選択肢として用意しているのです。

問いかけ	How did your meeting go?
不正解の応答例	I have an important meeting tomorrow.
正解の応答例	I think it went well.

Part 2 **Question-Response** 1-31〜34

最初に聞こえてくる英文に対する応答として最も適切なものを（A）〜（C）から選びましょう。

2. Mark your answer.　　（A）　　（B）　　（C）
3. Mark your answer.　　（A）　　（B）　　（C）
4. Mark your answer.　　（A）　　（B）　　（C）

Part 3 **解法のコツ**　　〈話者を問う設問〉

話し手の職業を尋ねる設問の場合、選択肢は職業名が並び、短いものが多いので、できるだけ会話を聞く前に選択肢まで見ておくようにしましょう。会話のヒントが得られます。また、"Who most likely is the woman?" のような質問は、職業名が選択肢に並ぶことが多いですが、「男性の同僚」のように、話し手との関係を示す選択肢が並ぶ場合もあるので注意しましょう。

・What is the woman's profession?
　（A）High school teacher
　（B）Lawyer
　（C）Professor
　（D）Medical doctor

> 短い選択肢が多いので、できれば事前に目を通しましょう。

Part 3 **Conversations** 1-35〜37

会話を聞き、5〜7の設問に対する解答として最も適切なものを（A）〜（D）から選びましょう。

5. What are the speakers talking about?

　（A）Their high school days
　（B）Their college days
　（C）Their children
　（D）Their current job

6. What is the woman's profession?

　（A）High school teacher
　（B）Lawyer
　（C）Professor
　（D）Medical doctor

7. Who is Mike?

　（A）Linda's husband
　（B）Their teacher
　（C）Jack's brother
　（D）The man's son

Part 4　解法のコツ　〈ラジオ放送〉

ラジオ放送には、下記のような基本的な流れがあるので、情報がどのような順序で出てくるか予測することができます。慣れておきましょう。

1. 挨拶、番組紹介　　You're listening to the morning show on Radio WACC.
　　　　　　　　　　⇒ラジオ局、番組名の紹介

2. 目的　　　　　　　Let's hear the traffic updates for today.
　　　　　　　　　　⇒交通情報の連絡

3. 詳細　　　　　　　Hudson Street will be temporarily closed from 1 P.M. till 5 P.M.
　　　　　　　　　　⇒道路閉鎖の案内

4. 次の情報の紹介　　Now, here's Susan Gilbert with our weekend weather report.
　　　　　　　　　　⇒次は天気予報

Part 4　Talks

 1-38～40

トークを聞き、8 ～ 10 の設問に対する解答として最も適切なものを（A）～（D）から選びましょう。

8. Who is this talk directed to?

(A) Radio station employees
(B) Radio listeners
(C) Moviegoers
(D) News reporters

9. What is John Cooper's program about?

(A) Weather
(B) Music
(C) Movies
(D) Poetry

10. Which program will be broadcast after this talk?

(A) Blast from the Past
(B) Poet's Corner
(C) The news and weather
(D) Traffic information

1. Part 2 のスクリプトにある最初の問いかけを使ってパートナーと英語で互いに質問をしてみましょう。質問に答える際は、下の回答例を参考にしましょう。なお、スクリプトは教員から配布されます。

Student A
Student B（パートナー）に Part 2 のスクリプトにある最初の問いかけをしてみましょう。

Student B
Student A（パートナー）の質問に対して下の回答例を参考に答えましょう。

Q2
・スマホでゲームを楽しんでいます。
・サッカーを楽しんでいます。
・友人と買い物を楽しんでいます。
・(You choose!)

Q3
・はい、両親と暮らしています。
・はい、両親、そして妹と暮らしています。
・いいえ、1人暮らしです。
・(You choose!)

Q4
・とても楽しかったです。
・あまり楽しくありませんでした。
・全然楽しくありませんでした。
・(You choose!)

2. Part 3 の対話スクリプトの内容について、パートナーと英語で互いに質問をしてみましょう。質問に答える際は、対話スクリプトだけを見るようにし、下の質問は見ないようにしましょう。なお、スクリプトは教員から配布されます。

Student A
Student B（パートナー）に下記の質問をしてみましょう。

Student B
Student A（パートナー）の質問に対して Part 3 の対話スクリプトを見ながら答えましょう。

1. What does the woman do?
2. Who is Jack?
3. Who plays basketball, Jack or Mike?
4. Does Jack want to become a lawyer?
5. (You choose!)

Reading Section

Part 5 / 解法のコツ 〈品詞問題 **3**〉

命令文などを除き、通常、英文には主語と（述語）動詞があります。品詞問題のうち名詞と動詞は、主語と（述語）動詞、そして目的語（動作の対象）という英文の基本要素を把握することが見分けるポイントです。

名　詞	人や物事などの名称を表し、主語や目的語となります。
動　詞	主語の動作や状態を示します。

⋮Check⋮

1 ～ 4 の英文中のカッコ内から正しい語を選び○で囲みましょう。

1. Brad has a terrible (memory / memorize) for names.
2. Let us know if you are unable to (attendance / attend).
3. (Sell / Sales) of automobiles are up this year.
4. The sales campaign was a big (succeed / success).

Part 5 / Incomplete Sentences

英文を完成させるのに最も適切な語句を（A）～（D）から選びましょう。

1. If the mixture seems dry, ------- water.

(A) additionally
(B) addition
(C) add
(D) additional

2. James never turns down an ------- to dinner.

(A) invitation
(B) inviting
(C) invitational
(D) invited

3. We will ------- our decision within a month.

(A) formal
(B) formally
(C) formality
(D) formalize

4. Please refer to our Web site for more ------- .

(A) informative
(B) information
(C) inform
(D) informatively

36

文挿入問題を除いて、Part 6 の問題形式は Part 5 と似ていますが、Part 5 と同様に空所を含む一文だけで解答可能な問題の他に、前後の文脈の理解が必要な問題も含まれています。こうした問題の場合、空所を含む文だけでは解答できないため、必ず直前・直後の文を読み文脈を確認しましょう。

Check

下線を引いた文に注意して、空所に当てはまる単語を（A）～（D）の中から選びましょう。

If you have any comments, feel free to let us know. Your ＿＿＿＿ is always welcome.

    (A) present

    (B) gift

    (C) stay

    (D) feedback

> この文だけでは正解にはたどり着けません。

Part 6　Text Completion

次の英文を読み、空所に入れるのに最も適切な語句や文を（A）～（D）から選びましょう。

Questions 5-8 refer to the following article.

Online shopping is a fast-growing market in the U.S. In a survey ------- in May last year, 40 percent of U.S.-based Internet users answered that they ------- goods online several times a month. ------- industry experts, there are several reasons why an increasing number of people are switching to shopping online. ------- . But the availability of massive discounts and coupons is also a major reason.

5.　(A) conduct
　　(B) conducting
　　(C) conducted
　　(D) conducts

6.　(A) bought
　　(B) made
　　(C) returned
　　(D) saw

7.　(A) In addition to
　　(B) On behalf of
　　(C) Despite
　　(D) According to

8.　(A) Buyers also rely on online reviews.
　　(B) Convenience remains the biggest factor.
　　(C) They prefer to buy in store.
　　(D) They don't often search online.

Part 7 　解法のコツ　〈チャット書式 1〉

Part 6 〜 7 では手紙やメモ、広告、通知など、様々な種類の文書が登場しますが、Part 7 特有な形式としてオンラインチャットが挙げられます。次のような指示文が記載され、1 〜 2 問出題されます。

> Questions 147-148 refer to the following text-message chain.

> Questions 161-164 refer to the following online discussion.

また、チャット特有の問題として、「〇時〇分に、●●さんは〜と書いているが、どういう意味か？」のように、チャットで使われた表現を引用し、話者の意図を尋ねるものがあります。

- At 17:14, what does Helena most likely mean when she writes, "No problem"?

引用された表現の文字どおりの意味ではなく、チャットのやりとりの中でどのように使われているかをよく考えて答えるようにしましょう。

Part 7 　Reading Comprehension

次の英文を読み、設問に対する答えとして最も適切なものを（A）〜（D）から選びましょう。

Questions 9-11 refer to the following text-message chain.

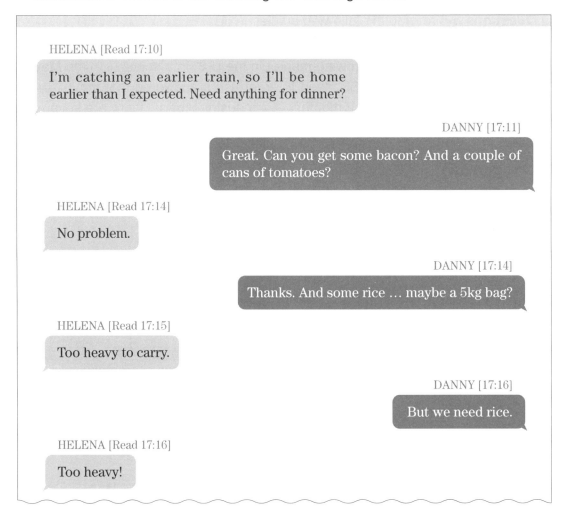

HELENA [Read 17:10]

I'm catching an earlier train, so I'll be home earlier than I expected. Need anything for dinner?

DANNY [17:11]

Great. Can you get some bacon? And a couple of cans of tomatoes?

HELENA [Read 17:14]

No problem.

DANNY [17:14]

Thanks. And some rice … maybe a 5kg bag?

HELENA [Read 17:15]

Too heavy to carry.

DANNY [17:16]

But we need rice.

HELENA [Read 17:16]

Too heavy!

DANNY [17:20]

Well, we need some other things too. How about I pick you up at the supermarket?

HELENA [Read 17:21]

That would be nice.

DANNY [17:23]

OK, let me know what time you want me to be there.

HELENA [17:26]

Train gets in at 5:47. See you at 6:00 in Freshmart?

9. At 17:14, what does Helena most likely mean when she writes, "No problem"?

(A) She has boarded her train.
(B) She is feeling much better.
(C) She can buy what Danny asked.
(D) She also likes bacon and tomatoes.

10. According to the chat, what is suggested about rice?

(A) Danny has just bought a 5kg bag of rice.
(B) Danny can do without rice for months.
(C) Helena tells Danny to buy it.
(D) Helena doesn't want to carry a 5kg bag of rice.

11. What will Danny most likely do at 6:00?

(A) Meet Helena at a supermarket
(B) Pick Helena up at a station
(C) Get off a train
(D) Buy food at a supermarket

Communicative Training

Part 7 で取り上げたチャットを使ってパートナーと英語で互いに質問をしてみましょう。答える際は、"Yes." や "No." だけで終わらないよう適宜、情報を追加しましょう。

Student A
Student B（パートナー）に下記の質問をしてみましょう。

Student B
Student A（パートナー）の質問に対してPart 7 の英文を見ながら答えましょう。

1. Who is taking an earlier train, Danny or Helena?
2. What does Danny ask Helena to buy?
3. Why doesn't Helena want to buy rice?
4. What does Danny suggest?
5. What time does Helena's train get in?
6. Where will they meet?
7. (You choose!)

UNIT 04 Personnel

 Vocabulary

1. 1 ～ 10 の語句の意味として適切なものを a ～ j の中から選びましょう。　　🎵 1-41

1. offer	_____		a.	支店、営業所
2. apply	_____		b.	感謝する
3. strict	_____		c.	会議
4. branch	_____		d.	申し出、提案
5. submit	_____		e.	申し込む
6. conference	_____		f.	資格、資質
7. work overtime	_____		g.	提出する
8. appreciate	_____		h.	登録
9. qualification	_____		i.	残業する
10. registration	_____		j.	厳しい

2. 語群の中から適切な日本語訳を選び、派生語の図を完成させましょう。

雇用　　雇用された　　従業員　　雇用主　　不注意に　　注意深く　　不注意な　　注意深い

 **Listening Section**

| Part 1 | 解法のコツ | 〈人物（3人以上）の描写1〉 |

3人以上の人物が写っている写真の場合、「彼らは全員〜している」のように、共通点を描写するものと、「1人の男性が〜している」のように、人物の中で目立つ人物を描写するタイプとに分かれます。They're で始まる文が聞こえた場合は、全員の共通点を描写しているかどうか確認しましょう。ただし、写真から全員の職業などが明らかな場合は、workers や travelers のような具体的な単語が主語として使われることもあります。

Check

1〜6の単語とその日本語訳とを線で結びましょう。

　　1. passenger ・　　　　　　　・食事客

　　2. server ・　　　　　　　　・観光旅行者

　　3. mechanic ・　　　　　　　・買い物客

　　4. diner ・　　　　　　　　　・乗客

　　5. tourist ・　　　　　　　　・機械工

　　6. shopper ・　　　　　　　　・給仕係

| Part 1 | Photographs |

 1-42, 43

（A）〜（D）の英文を聞き、写真を最も適切に描写しているものを選びましょう。

1.

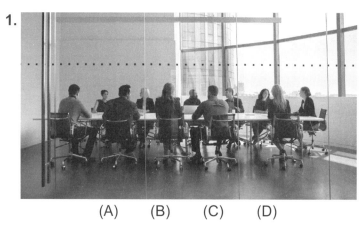

　　　　（A）　　　（B）　　　（C）　　　（D）

| Part 2 | 解法のコツ | 〈否定疑問文〉 |

Yes/No 疑問文の中には、"Don't you like it?" のように文頭が否定語で始まる否定疑問文があります。日本語だと「はい、好きではありません」と答えられますが、英語の場合は、通常の疑問文であろうと否定疑問文であろうと、肯定するなら Yes、否定するなら No と答えると覚えておきましょう。

　　問いかけ　　　　Aren't you coming with us?

　　不正解の応答例　Yes, I'm not going.

　　正解の応答例　　No, I'm busy now.

1-44〜47

最初に聞こえてくる英文に対する応答として最も適切なものを（A）〜（C）から選びましょう。

2. Mark your answer.   (A)   (B)   (C)
3. Mark your answer.   (A)   (B)   (C)
4. Mark your answer.   (A)   (B)   (C)

Part 3   解法のコツ   〈時を問う設問〉

時を尋ねる設問では、"When will the interview begin?" のように when で始まるものが定番ですが、この他にも how often や how soon など様々な疑問詞を使って尋ねられることがあるので慣れておきましょう。

- <u>How often</u> does the bus run?   ⇒「どのくらいの間隔」で頻度がポイント！
- <u>How long</u> has the man been waiting?   ⇒「どのくらい」で時間の長さがポイント！
- <u>How soon</u> does the show begin?   ⇒「どのくらいすぐ」で開始時期がポイント！
- <u>How long ago</u> did the man order?   ⇒「どのくらい前」で過去の時期がポイント！

Part 3   Conversations

 1-48〜50

会話を聞き、5〜7の設問に対する解答として最も適切なものを（A）〜（D）から選びましょう。

5. What are the speakers talking about?

(A) Their language ability
(B) A sales meeting
(C) Applications for a job opening
(D) Their new position

6. What is going to be hard work?

(A) To apply for a sales position
(B) To select applicants
(C) To choose a new career
(D) To become bilingual

7. When will they meet?

(A) After lunch today
(B) After the meeting today
(C) Tomorrow morning
(D) At one o'clock tomorrow

Part 4　解法のコツ　〈社内アナウンス〉

社内アナウンスには、下記のような基本的な流れがあるので、情報がどのような順序で出てくるか予測することができます。慣れておきましょう。

1. 挨拶	Good morning.	
2. 目的	I have a hiring update for everyone.	⇒採用に関する最新情報の連絡
3. 詳細	Robert Olson will begin working next Monday.	⇒新入社員の紹介
4. 追加情報	On Monday, Cathy Baker will give him an orientation.	⇒オリエンテーションの連絡
5. 結び	Thank you.	

Part 4　Talks

 1-51〜53

トークを聞き、8 〜 10 の設問に対する解答として最も適切なものを（A）〜（D）から選びましょう。

8. What is the purpose of this talk?

(A) To introduce a new member
(B) To announce the opening of a new branch
(C) To explain a new financial system
(D) To close a meeting

9. Who is Nick Steel?

(A) A judge
(B) A financial adviser
(C) A director
(D) A salesperson

10. What will Nick most likely do next?

(A) Make a farewell speech
(B) Explain the Denver branch's profitability
(C) Ask a few questions
(D) Introduce himself

Communicative Training

1. Part 2 のスクリプトにある最初の問いかけを使ってパートナーと英語で互いに質問をして
みましょう。質問に答える際は、下の回答例を参考にしましょう。なお、スクリプトは教
員から配布されます。

Student A
Student B（パート
ナー）に Part 2 の
スクリプトにある最
初の問いかけをして
みましょう。

Student B
Student A（パート
ナー）の質問に対し
て下の回答例を参考
に答えましょう。

Q2
・はい、そう思います。
・よくわかりません。
・いいえ、そうは思いませ
ん。
・(You choose!)

Q3
・はい、しました。
・はい、昨日応募しました。
・いいえ、興味がありませ
んでした。
・(You choose!)

Q4
・ええ、昨日彼に会いました。
・本当ですか？ 彼について
教えてください。
・そうですか？ 知りません
でした。
・(You choose!)

2. Part 4 のスクリプトの内容について、パートナーと英語で互いに質問をしてみましょう。
質問に答える際は、スクリプトだけを見るようにし、下の質問は見ないようにしましょう。
なお、スクリプトは教員から配布されます。

Student A
Student B（パート
ナー）に下記の質問
をしてみましょう。

Student B
Student A（パート
ナー）の質問に対し
て Part 4 のスクリ
プトを見ながら答え
ましょう。

1. Who is Nick Steel?
2. When did Nick join his current office?
3. Where did he work before that?
4. What helped improve the Denver branch's profitability?
5. (You choose!)

Reading Section

選択肢に目を通し、(take / have taken / taking / took) のように、ある動詞の活用形が並んでいる場合は、動詞の形を問う問題です。動詞の形を問う問題は、時制を問うものと、態（受動態かそれとも能動態か）を問うものの 2 種類に分けられますが、時制の場合、時を表す語句（now や last night など）が決め手になります。

✦Check✦

次の 1～6 の英文と、その英文中の動詞が示す時制とを線で結びましょう。

1. Ryan is talking on the phone right now. •
2. Sam has just finished his presentation. •
3. We'll see him at the conference next week. •
4. I've been working on the report for five days. •
5. Beth usually leaves the office at five. •

6. I attended that workshop two days ago. •

• 現在形（いつものこと・習慣）
• 現在進行形（今している動作）
• 過去形（終わったこと）
• 未来形（これからのこと）
• 現在完了形（過去とつながりのある現在の状態。完了や経験、継続を表す）

• 現在完了進行形（ずっと続いている動作）

Part 5 Incomplete Sentences

英文を完成させるのに最も適切な語句を（A）～（D）から選びましょう。

1. Our sales ------- by five percent last year.

(A) increases
(B) increased
(C) is increasing
(D) have increased

2. I usually ------- off work at five, but I have to work overtime today.

(A) get
(B) am getting
(C) have gotten
(D) gotten

3. This new product ------- to sell well.

(A) expects
(B) expected
(C) is expected
(D) is expecting

4. Hurry! The boss ------- for you since this morning.

(A) waits
(B) waited
(C) will wait
(D) has been waiting

文脈の理解が必要となる問題では、「しかし」や「したがって」のように、2 つの文をつなぐ副詞（句）を選ばせるものが登場します。これらの副詞（句）は、読解の際に非常に重要ですから確実にマスターしておきましょう。

Check

語群から適切な語句を書き入れ、表を完成させましょう。

結果（したがって、そのため）	逆接（しかし、それでもなお）	情報追加（さらに、しかも）
therefore		

語群

> in addition, however, ✓ therefore, moreover, nevertheless, as a result, thus

Part 6 Text Completion

次の英文を読み、空所に入れるのに最も適切な語句や文を（A）〜（D）から選びましょう。

Questions 5-8 refer to the following e-mail.

From: Kate Harris <kateharris@bigone.com>
To: Sally James <sallyjames@gmail.com>
Date: June 12, 2022
Subject: Your Application for Big One Sporting Goods, Inc.

Dear Ms. James,

We appreciate your ------- for the position of Marketing Assistant at Big One Sporting Goods, Inc.
5.

Unfortunately, in the recruiting process, we have decided to hire another applicant whose qualifications were better suited to ------- needs. ------- , we will not be offering you the position.
6.   7.

Thank you for your interest in our company. ------- .
8.

Sincerely yours,

Kate Harris
Manager
Human Resources Division
Big One Sporting Goods, Inc.

5. (A) apply
(B) applicant
(C) application
(D) applicable

6. (A) your
(B) our
(C) you
(D) us

7. (A) However
(B) In addition
(C) Nevertheless
(D) As a result

8. (A) We wish you the best in the future.
(B) We hope to see you next week.
(C) I'm sure you will enjoy working with us.
(D) You're the right person for the position.

指定の文に対して最も適した挿入箇所を選ぶ「文挿入問題」は、前後の文脈を見極めなければならず、他の問題に比べて難易度が高いです。そのため、解答するのを最後に回すのも 1 つの手です。また、文挿入問題は次のような形式なので、慣れておきましょう。

10. In which of the positions marked [1], [2], [3], and [4] does the following sentence best belong?

"I'm sure she'll do well in her new position."

(A) [1]

(B) [2]

この文が入る適切な位置を [1] 〜 [4] から選びます。

(C) [3]

(D) [4]

Part 7 Reading Comprehension

次の英文を読み、設問に対する答えとして最も適切なものを（A）〜（D）から選びましょう。

Questions 9-12 refer to the following notice.

FRANCHISE SUPPORT WORKSHOPS

Our bimonthly Legal Affairs Training Workshops will resume from next month. — [1] —.

If you are concerned about the latest changes in the tax law, or if you are unclear about your tax obligations as an employer, our April workshop aims to answer your questions. — [2] —.

The workshop theme is not yet determined. — [3] —. Please submit your questions and requests as part of the registration process no later than one week before the workshop. A link to the registration form is provided below. — [4] —.

Cost: Free to members. Non-members $40 (inc. tax).
Time & Date: 7:00 P.M., April 15
Venue: Landon Park Hotel, Benson Ave. Springfield
Registration deadline: April 8
URL: https://www.franchisesupport.com

Note: Participants will be limited to 20.

9. For whom is the notice most likely intended?

    (A) Franchise employees
    (B) Franchise business owners
    (C) Lawyers
    (D) Law students

10. What should people do if they want to attend the workshop?

    (A) Visit Landon Park Hotel
    (B) Send an e-mail
    (C) Make a telephone call
    (D) Submit a form online

11. What is true about the workshop?

    (A) Up to 20 people can attend it.
    (B) It is only open to members.
    (C) It will be held in the morning.
    (D) It is held twice a month.

12. In which of the positions marked [1], [2], [3], and [4] does the following sentence best belong?
"It will depend on issues raised by participants."

    (A) [1]
    (B) [2]
    (C) [3]
    (D) [4]

Communicative Training

Part 7 で取り上げた告知文を使ってパートナーと英語で互いに質問をしてみましょう。答える際は、"Yes." や "No." だけで終わらないよう適宜、情報を追加しましょう。

Student A
Student B（パートナー）に下記の質問をしてみましょう。

Student B
Student A（パートナー）の質問に対して Part 7 の英文を見ながら答えましょう。

1. How often is the workshop held?
2. Where will the workshop be held?
3. What is the theme of the workshop?
4. Can non-members attend the workshop?
5. When is the deadline for registration?
6. How many people can attend the workshop?
7. (You choose!)

本テキストで取り上げている接尾辞一覧 1

　接尾辞とは、specialist の -ist など、語の後ろに付けられる要素を指します。接尾辞を付けることにより品詞が変化することが多く、接尾辞を見ると品詞が推測できます。例えば exist（存在する）という動詞の後ろに -ence が付くことにより existence（存在）という名詞になります。次の表を使って本テキストで取り上げている名詞を作る接尾辞を確認しましょう。

名詞を作る接尾辞

接尾辞	意味		例
-ant	人	～する人	applicant（応募者）（< apply）
-ee		～される人	employee（従業員）（< employ）
-er		～する人	employer（雇用主）（< employ）
-ian		～する人	magician（手品師）（< magic）
-ist		～な人、～する人	specialist（専門家）（< special）
-or		～する人	educator（教育者）（< educate）
-ence	こと、状態		existence（存在）（< exist）
-ion, -sion, -tion			invention（発明）（< invent）
-ity, -ty			security（安全）（< secure）
-ment			excitement（興奮）（< excite）
-ness			politeness（礼儀正しさ）（< polite）
-th			width（広さ）（< wide）

-er（～する人）
interviewer
（面接官、インタビューアー）

interview
面接する

-ee（～される人）
interviewee
（面接を受ける人、受験者）

UNIT 05 Shopping

 Vocabulary

1. 1 ～ 10 の語句の意味として適切なものを a ～ j の中から選びましょう。　🎧 1-54

1. suitable	_____	a. 協力
2. purchase	_____	b.（当然のこととして～を）要求する
3. refund	_____	c. ふさわしい、適切な
4. item	_____	d. 記念日
5. replace	_____	e. 返金
6. cooperation	_____	f. 商品、品物
7. anniversary	_____	g.（物が）利用可能な、入手できる
8. valid	_____	h. 購入（品）、購入する
9. claim	_____	i.（チケットなどが）有効な
10. available	_____	j. ～を取り換える

2. 語群の中から適切な日本語訳を選び、派生語の図を完成させましょう。

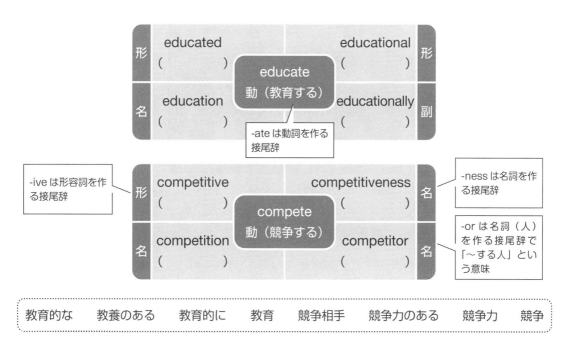

| 形 | educated （　　　） | | educational （　　　） | 形 |
| 名 | education （　　　） | educate 動（教育する） | educationally （　　　） | 副 |

-ate は動詞を作る接尾辞

-ive は形容詞を作る接尾辞

-ness は名詞を作る接尾辞

| 形 | competitive （　　　） | | competitiveness （　　　） | 名 |
| 名 | competition （　　　） | compete 動（競争する） | competitor （　　　） | 名 |

-or は名詞（人）を作る接尾辞で「～する人」という意味

教育的な　　教養のある　　教育的に　　教育　　競争相手　　競争力のある　　競争力　　競争

Listening Section

Part 1 　解法のコツ　〈風景の描写〉

風景写真の場合、まずどのような場所かを把握しましょう。また、人物写真の場合と違い、選択肢の主語がすべて異なることも多いので、写真と照合しながら聞き取りましょう。また、人がいないことを示す unoccupied や empty などの表現にも慣れておきましょう。

The desks are unoccupied.
（机には誰も座っていません）

The street is empty.
（通りには人通りがありません）

Part 1 　**Photographs**　　　　　　　　　　　　　　　　🎧 1-55, 56

（A）〜（D）の英文を聞き、写真を最も適切に描写しているものを選びましょう。

1.

（A）　　（B）　　（C）　　（D）

Part 2 　解法のコツ　〈選択疑問文〉

"A or B?" という形式の選択疑問文は Yes/No では答えられないので、Yes/No で始まる選択肢は不正解となります。基本的には A か B のどちらかを選ぶ応答が正解になりますが、「どちらでも良いです」のような応答が正解になることもあります。

　　問いかけ　　　　Which would you prefer, tea or coffee?
　　正解の応答例　　Either is fine.

最初に聞こえてくる英文に対する応答として最も適切なものを（A）～（C）から選びましょう。

2. Mark your answer.　　　(A)　　　(B)　　　(C)
3. Mark your answer.　　　(A)　　　(B)　　　(C)
4. Mark your answer.　　　(A)　　　(B)　　　(C)

Part 3 **解法のコツ** 　〈次の行動を問う設問〉

"What will the man probably do next?" のように、会話の後に話し手がどのような行動をするかを問う設問は頻出問題の１つです。３つある設問のうち最後の設問として登場することが多く、会話における最後の発言がポイントになるので、注意して聞き取りましょう。

・What will the man probably do next?
・What does the man ask the woman to do?
・What does the man say he will do?
・What is the man told to do?

> 会話の最後で何と言っているかに注意しましょう！

Part 3 **Conversations** 1-61～63

会話を聞き、５～７の設問に対する解答として最も適切なものを（A）～（D）から選びましょう。

5. Where is the woman going this weekend?

(A) To a shopping mall
(B) To a formal party
(C) To a casual party
(D) To a fitting room

6. What will the woman probably buy?

(A) A skirt
(B) A sweater
(C) A formal suit
(D) A dress

7. What will the woman probably do next?

(A) Try on the dress
(B) Try on the sweater
(C) Go to a different store
(D) Go to a party

Part 4   解法のコツ   〈店内アナウンス〉

店内アナウンスには、下記のような基本的な流れがあるので、情報がどのような順序で出てくるか予測することができます。慣れておきましょう。

1. 呼びかけ	Attention all customers! ⇒対象は顧客
2. 目的	The store will close in 15 minutes. Please take all your purchases to the cashier now. ⇒閉店時間のお知らせ
3. 追加情報、注意事項	If you are buying five or fewer items and are paying with cash, you can use the express checkout lane. ⇒エクスプレスレジの案内
4. 結び	Thank you for shopping with us today. ⇒謝辞

Part 4   Talks

 1-64〜66

トークを聞き、8 〜 10 の設問に対する解答として最も適切なものを（A）〜（D）から選びましょう。

8. What is this announcement about?

(A) Free entertainment
(B) Coupons for a free dessert
(C) Discount tickets
(D) New restaurants

9. What is Blue River Mall celebrating?

(A) The opening of the mall
(B) Its 5th anniversary
(C) A major upgrade
(D) Its 15th anniversary

10. Where can you get your coupon?

(A) At information desks
(B) At 4th floor restaurants
(C) At the basement food court
(D) At any store in Blue River Mall

1. Part 2 のスクリプトにある最初の問いかけを使ってパートナーと英語で互いに質問をしてみましょう。質問に答える際は、下の回答例を参考にしましょう。なお、スクリプトは教員から配布されます。

Student A
Student B（パートナー）に Part 2 のスクリプトにある最初の問いかけをしてみましょう。

Student B
Student A（パートナー）の質問に対して下の回答例を参考に答えましょう。

Q2
・それは月曜日に閉まっています。
・すみません、わかりません。
・どちらでもありません。日曜が定休日です（日曜日に閉まっています）。
・（You choose!）

Q3
・現金で支払います。
・クレジットカードで支払います。
・これは使えますか？
・（You choose!）

Q4
・この青いジャケットのほうです。
・他のジャケットを見てもよいですか？
・どちらでもよいです。
・（You choose!）

2. Part 3 の対話スクリプトの内容について、パートナーと英語で互いに質問をしてみましょう。質問に答える際は、対話スクリプトだけを見るようにし、下の質問は見ないようにしましょう。なお、スクリプトは教員から配布されます。

Student A
Student B（パートナー）に下記の質問をしてみましょう。

Student B
Student A（パートナー）の質問に対して Part 3 の対話スクリプトを見ながら答えましょう。

1. What does the man say about the sweater?
2. What does the woman need for the party this weekend?
3. Is that a formal party or a casual one?
4. Is she going to try on the black dress?
5. (You choose!)

Part 5 　解法のコツ　　〈動詞の形問題 2〉

動詞の形を問う問題は時制を問うものが中心ですが、態（受動態かそれとも能動態か）を問うものも含まれます。受動態かそれとも能動態かを問うだけであれば 2 択ですが、実際の問題では選択肢が 4 つありますので、惑わされないようにしましょう。

能動態	「～は…する」のように、何かに働きかける意味を表します。 ex.) One of the interns **made** the mistake.
受動態	「～は…される／されている」のように、何らかの動作を受ける意味を表します。 ex.) The mistake **was made** by one of the interns.

⸉Check⸊

1 ～ 4 の英文中のカッコ内から正しい語句を選び○で囲みましょう。

1. The store (cleans / is cleaned) every morning.

2. We will (open / be opened) our online store next month.

3. The meeting will (hold / be held) here.

4. My new tablet (fell / was fallen) off the table and broke.

Part 5　Incomplete Sentences

英文を完成させるのに最も適切な語句を（A）～（D）から選びましょう。

1. A clearance sale ------- next week at this store.

    (A) schedules
    (B) scheduling
    (C) is scheduled
    (D) is scheduling

2. All the staff members must ------- uniforms at this store.

    (A) be worn
    (B) wearing
    (C) worn
    (D) wear

3. My credit card ------- while I was shopping at the mall.

    (A) was stolen
    (B) will steal
    (C) stole
    (D) was stealing

4. All items can ------- for a refund within seven days of purchase.

    (A) return
    (B) be returned
    (C) returning
    (D) returned

2 つの文をつなぐ副詞（句）では、すでに取り上げた「結果」、「逆接」、「情報追加」に加えて、「例示」、「順序」、「条件」などもよく登場するので、これらについても確認しておきましょう。

⟩Check⟨

語群から適切な語句を書き入れ、表を完成させましょう。

例示（例えば）	順序（まず、それから、最後に）	条件（さもなければ）
	first	

語群

> finally,　for example,　otherwise,　✓first,　next,　for instance,　then

Part 6　Text Completion

次の英文を読み、空所に入れるのに最も適切な語句や文を（A）〜（D）から選びましょう。

Questions 5-8 refer to the following article.

Mark's Donuts is the world's favorite brand of donuts and coffee. They also have a Web site where you can ------- freshly baked donuts, coffee, as well as coffee powder and mixes. ------- , Mark's Donuts has a broad selection of collectibles that can also ------- online. ------- .
5.　　　　　　　　　　　　　　6.　　　　　　　　　　　　7.　　　　　　8.

5. (A) eat
   (B) order
   (C) bring
   (D) invent

6. (A) Otherwise
   (B) First
   (C) Additionally
   (D) However

7. (A) be purchased
   (B) purchase
   (C) purchased
   (D) purchasing

8. (A) Mark's Donuts closed last month.
   (B) You need to buy them at your local Mark's Donuts store.
   (C) They do not have their own Web site.
   (D) Go to www.marksdonuts.com for more details.

Part 7 では限られた時間で大量の英文を読まなければならないので、文書を読む前に設問を読んでおき、解答に必要な情報だけを探すつもりで文書を読んでいく必要があります。その際、次に挙げるような設問の場合、A にあたる語句がキーワードになるので、文書を読む際には A を探し、そこに書かれている内容を素早く読み取りましょう。

・What is indicated about A?
・What is stated about A?
・What is true about A?
・What is suggested about A?

いずれも A に関して書かれていることを探しましょう！

Part 7　Reading Comprehension

次の英文を読み、設問に対する答えとして最も適切なものを（A）～（D）から選びましょう。

Questions 9-12 refer to the following e-mail.

From:	graham@printerjoes.com
To:	pipeson.m@enterprise.com
Subject:	Your order (PJ24673207)
Date:	November 28, 1:30 P.M.

Dear Ms. Pipeson,

Thank you very much for your recent purchase from Printer Joe's.
We have confirmed that you have submitted the data for the following order.

File name:　　 History of Language.pdf
Order number: PJ24673207
Item name:　　 Pamphlet

As long as there is no problem with the data, we will ship the order on the following date.
Estimated shipping date: December 1 (evening)

You can replace or re-submit your Web-submitted data from your "My Page" at any time until we issue the "Data Check Complete" report. The use of the data re-submission window is only available once. If you wish to replace the data again after re-submitting it, please contact our customer center at 555-2150.

Thank you for your cooperation.

Printer Joe's
Online Printing & Publishing

9. What is the purpose of the e-mail?

(A) To issue a report
(B) To confirm an order
(C) To answer a question about an order
(D) To cancel an online purchase

10. What should Ms. Pipeson do if she wants to replace the data after re-submitting it?

(A) Call 555-2150
(B) Send an e-mail to the customer center
(C) Submit a complaint form from her "My Page"
(D) Open the data re-submission window

11. The word "issue" in paragraph 4, line 2, is closest in meaning to

(A) keep
(B) receive
(C) request
(D) send

12. What is stated about the "Data Check Complete" report?

(A) It can be revised from Ms. Pipeson's "My Page."
(B) It can be used to make a purchase.
(C) It has been submitted to Ms. Pipeson.
(D) It will be issued by Printer Joe's.

Communicative Training

Part 7 で取り上げた e メールを使ってパートナーと英語で互いに質問をしてみましょう。答える際は、"Yes." や "No." だけで終わらないよう適宜、情報を追加しましょう。

Student A
Student B（パートナー）に下記の質問をしてみましょう。

Student B
Student A（パートナー）の質問に対して Part 7 の英文を見ながら答えましょう。

1. What is Printer Joe's?
2. Who is this message intended for?
3. Has Printer Joe's shipped the order yet?
4. When is the order estimated to be shipped?
5. How many times can the data re-submission window be opened?
6. Who will issue the "Data Check Complete" report, Ms. Pipeson or Printer Joe's?
7. (You choose!)

本テキストで取り上げている接尾辞一覧 2

　接尾辞の中には、動詞や名詞の後ろに付いて形容詞を作るものがいろいろあります。例えば imagine（想像する）という動詞の後ろに -able がつくことにより imaginable（想像できる）という形容詞になります。次の表を使って本テキストで取り上げている形容詞を作る接尾辞を確認しましょう。

形容詞を作る接尾辞

接尾辞	意味	例
-able	～できる	imaginable（想像できる）（< imagine）
-al	～の	additional（追加の）（< addition）
-ed	～された	satisfied（満足した）（< satisfy）
-ent	～な	excellent（極めて優れた）（< excel）
-ful	～に満ちた	careful（注意深い）（< care）
-ing	～させるような、～している	exciting（興奮させるような）（< excite）
-ive	～な	active（活動的な）（< act）
-less	～のない	careless（不注意な）（< care）
-ory	～な	satisfactory（満足できる）（< satisfy）
-ous	～な	dangerous（危険な）（< danger）

-ful（～に満ちた）
painful（痛い、痛みを伴う）

pain
痛み

-less（～のない）
painless（痛みのない）

-ing（～させるような）
boring（退屈な）

bore
退屈させる

-ed（～された）
bored（退屈した）

Finances

UNIT 06

 Vocabulary

1. 1 〜 10 の語句の意味として適切なものを a 〜 j の中から選びましょう。　　🎧 1-67

1. purse	_____	a. 維持管理、保守
2. raise	_____	b. 年金
3. maintenance	_____	c.（金額などが）妥当な、高くない
4. property	_____	d. 昇給
5. reasonable	_____	e. 資産
6. ceremony	_____	f. 料金、手数料
7. account	_____	g. 財布、ハンドバック
8. pension	_____	h. 口座、取引
9. investment	_____	i. 投資
10. charge	_____	j. 式典

2. 語群の中から適切な日本語訳を選び、派生語の図を完成させましょう。

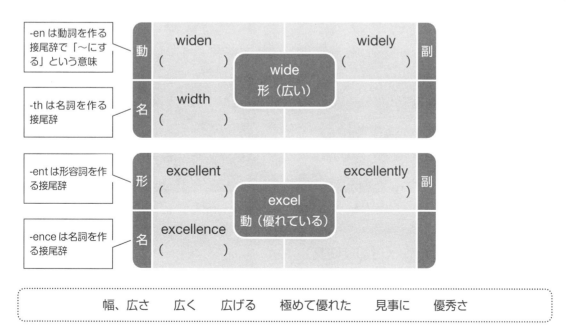

-en は動詞を作る接尾辞で「〜にする」という意味

-th は名詞を作る接尾辞

動　widen　（　　　）

名　width　（　　　）

wide
形（広い）

widely　（　　　）　副

-ent は形容詞を作る接尾辞

-ence は名詞を作る接尾辞

形　excellent　（　　　）

名　excellence　（　　　）

excel
動（優れている）

excellently　（　　　）　副

幅、広さ　　広く　　広げる　　極めて優れた　　見事に　　優秀さ

61

Listening Section

Part 1 | 解法のコツ | 〈現在進行形〉

人物写真の場合、その人の「動作」と「状態」を描写するのに現在進行形が多く使われます。〈am/is/are+動詞の ing 形〉の部分だけでなく、その後に続く目的語までセットで聞き取るようにしましょう。

✦Check✦

下の写真の描写として最も適切な英文を 1 ～ 4 の中から選びましょう。

1. The man is taking a deep breath.
2. The man is taking a nap.
3. The man is taking a walk.
4. The man is taking pictures.

> 動詞部分はすべて同じであり、正答の決め手になるのは下線部の目的語です。

Part 1 | **Photographs**

 1-68, 69

(A) ～ (D) の英文を聞き、写真を最も適切に描写しているものを選びましょう。

1.

(A)　　(B)　　(C)　　(D)

Part 2 | 解法のコツ | 〈付加疑問文〉

「～ですよね？」のように、相手に同意を求めたり、念を押したりする疑問文（付加疑問文）の答え方は、基本的に Yes/No 疑問文と同じです。

問いかけ　　You were here this morning, weren't you?

正解の応答例　　No, I went to the dentist.

最初に聞こえてくる英文に対する応答として最も適切なものを（A）〜（C）から選びましょう。

2. Mark your answer.　　　(A)　　　(B)　　　(C)
3. Mark your answer.　　　(A)　　　(B)　　　(C)
4. Mark your answer.　　　(A)　　　(B)　　　(C)

Part 3 **解法のコツ**　　〈図表問題 1〉

図表を見ながら解答する問題では、設問を先に読む際に図表にも目を通しておきましょう。3 つの設問のうち図表に関するものは基本的に 1 つで、"Look at the graphic." という指示文が設問の始めに書かれています。

図表を見て答える問題を示しています。

Lecture Schedule

Time	Topic
11:00 A.M.	Security in the Home
1:00 P.M.	Investing in Property
3:00 P.M.	Housing Loans
5:00 P.M.	Home Renovation

6. Look at the graphic. What talk will the speakers probably go to first?

　(A) Security in the Home
　(B) Investing in Property
　(C) Housing Loans
　(D) Home Renovation

Part 3 **Conversations** 1-74〜76

会話を聞き、5 〜 7 の設問に対する解答として最も適切なものを（A）〜（D）から選びましょう。

Lecture Schedule

Time	Topic
11:00 A.M.	Security in the Home
1:00 P.M.	Investing in Property
3:00 P.M.	Housing Loans
5:00 P.M.	Home Renovation

5. How many lectures will the speakers probably attend?

　(A) One
　(B) Two
　(C) Three
　(D) Four

6. Look at the graphic. What talk will the speakers probably go to first?

　(A) Security in the Home
　(B) Investing in Property
　(C) Housing Loans
　(D) Home Renovation

7. When will the speakers most likely meet?

　(A) 10:30
　(B) 11:00
　(C) 12:30
　(D) 1:00

設問は、「何についてのメッセージですか？」のような概要に関する設問と、「講演は何時に終わりますか？」のような細かい内容に関する設問の2つに分かれます。また、多くの場合、3つの設問のうち第1問は概要に関する設問で、第2～3問が細かい内容に関する設問となっています。その場合、設問はトークの流れに沿って出題されるので、第2問はトークの前半、第3問は後半に関連していると考えてよいでしょう。

Part 4 　Talks 1-77～79

トークを聞き、8～10の設問に対する解答として最も適切なものを（A）～（D）から選びましょう。

8. What is this talk about?

    (A) A salary cut
    (B) Next month's salary
    (C) Job losses
    (D) A delay in payment

9. According to the speaker, what caused the problem?

    (A) A system shutdown
    (B) Slow sales
    (C) Yesterday's election
    (D) Lack of finance

10. When will the payment be made?

    (A) On the 16th
    (B) On the 17th
    (C) By the end of this month
    (D) By the end of next month

Communicative Training

1. Part 2 のスクリプトにある最初の問いかけを使ってパートナーと英語で互いに質問をしてみましょう。質問に答える際は、下の回答例を参考にしましょう。なお、スクリプトは教員から配布されます。

Student A
Student B（パートナー）に Part 2 のスクリプトにある最初の問いかけをしてみましょう。

Student B
Student A（パートナー）の質問に対して下の回答例を参考に答えましょう。

Q2
- 私はいつも現金を持ち歩きます。
- 現金は持ち歩きません。
- クレジットカードでいつも支払います。
- (You choose!)

Q3
- はい、そうです。
- いいえ、私は昇給しませんでした。
- いいえ、（私ではなく）彼が昇給しました。
- (You choose!)

Q4
- はい、私たちの予算はとても厳しいです。
- いいえ、私たちには大きな予算があります。
- 本当ですか？　予算については何も知りません。
- (You choose!)

---

2. Part 3 の対話スクリプトの内容について、パートナーと英語で互いに質問をしてみましょう。質問に答える際は、対話スクリプトだけを見るようにし、下の質問は見ないようにしましょう。なお、スクリプトは教員から配布されます。

Student A
Student B（パートナー）に下記の質問をしてみましょう。

Student B
Student A（パートナー）の質問に対して Part 3 の対話スクリプトを見ながら答えましょう。

1. What time does the talk on Housing Loans begin?
2. Is the woman interested in the morning talk?
3. How many talks are the man and the woman going to?
4. When and where are they going to meet?
5. (You choose!)

Part 5 　解法のコツ 　〈語彙問題〉

選択肢に目を通し、(short / small / close / tall) のように、同じ品詞の単語が並んでいる場合は、語彙の知識を問う「語彙問題」です。語彙問題も品詞問題と同様によく出題されますが、① food と meal、menu のように、意味の似た単語、② object と reject、eject のように形の似た単語という２つのパターンがあるので注意しておきましょう。

⸜Check⸝

1～3 の英文中のカッコ内から正しい語を選び○で囲みましょう。

　　1. Donald ordered a chicken dish from the (food / meal / menu).
　　2. Do you (object / reject / eject) to our decision?
　　3. Our professor (said / told / talked) us to finish the homework.

Part 5 　**Incomplete Sentences**

英文を完成させるのに最も適切な語句を（A）～（D）から選びましょう。

1. The next step is to ------- finance to develop the project.

　　(A) contain
　　(B) rely
　　(C) obtain
　　(D) reply

2. You'll find some money in my ------- .

　　(A) purse
　　(B) pursuit
　　(C) purchase
　　(D) purpose

3. We decorated our house on a ------- budget.

　　(A) little
　　(B) light
　　(C) short
　　(D) tight

4. Paul drew some money out of his ------- to pay for his son's trip to Italy.

　　(A) control
　　(B) account
　　(C) discount
　　(D) mind

イベントの発表、告知などを扱った英文では、「〜をお知らせいたします」や「〜で開催されます」のような定型表現が数多く出てきます。こうした定型表現が語句挿入の問題に使われることもあるので、ぜひ慣れておきましょう。

Check

1〜4の英文中で下線を引いた語句とその日本語訳とを線で結びましょう。

1. Macy's <u>is pleased to announce</u> the opening of its new store. •   • 開催される
2. Visitors <u>are encouraged to use</u> public transportation. •   • 〜を呼びものとする
3. The concert <u>takes place</u> next Thursday. •   • 〜を発表いたします
4. His latest movie <u>features</u> an all-star cast. •   • 〜をご利用ください

Part 6 Text Completion

次の英文を読み、空所に入れるのに最も適切な語句や文を（A）〜（D）から選びましょう。

Questions 5-8 refer to the following announcement.

ABC Union Bank

is pleased to invite Austin residents to
the official Grand Opening celebration of ------- new bank branch
5.
in Austin, Texas. The ribbon cutting ceremony ------- place at 11:00 A.M.
6.
on Monday, Feb. 11 at 2535 West Anderson Drive.
The ribbon cutting ceremony will feature refreshments and live ------- .
7.
Austin Mayor Scott Evans and CEO of ABC Union Bank Larry Smith will speak
at the celebratory event. ------- .
8.

---

5. (A) your
   (B) its
   (C) my
   (D) his

6. (A) took
   (B) was taking
   (C) will take
   (D) take

7. (A) entertain
   (B) entertaining
   (C) entertainer
   (D) entertainment

8. (A) Austin locals are encouraged to attend the free Grand Opening festivities.
   (B) Austin is known for great live music venues.
   (C) ABC Union Bank is currently seeking a sales manager.
   (D) The event turned out to be a great success.

eメールと並び、手紙もよく出題される文書形式の1つです。eメールと似ていますが、レターヘッドからeメールよりも多くの情報を得ることができます。次の書式例で特徴に慣れておきましょう。

手紙の書式例

Happy Travel

5160 S. Valley View
Blvd. #112, Las Vegas,
NV 89118

Mr. Dave Smith
7935 Badura Ave #1035
Las Vegas, NV 89113

July 21

Dear Mr. Smith,

_____
_____
_____
_____
_____

Sincerely,

John Wilson

John Wilson
Happy Travel

Enclosure

■レターヘッド
差出人の会社名、住所、電話番号などが記されます。

■宛先の氏名・住所
宛先の氏名、住所が記されます。

■日付

■本文
最初に、宛名が記されます。
次に、用件が述べられますが、多くの場合、「導入⇒本論⇒結論」という流れになります。

結びは、(Yours) Sincerely のほか、(Best) Regards などもよく使われます。

■差出人の署名等
差出人の署名、氏名、所属（役職、部署、会社名など）が記されます。

■同封物の有無

次の英文を読み、設問に対する答えとして最も適切なものを（A）〜（D）から選びましょう。

Questions 9-12 refer to the following letter.

Walters International

Nexus Building 20th Floor, 41 Connaught Road Central,
Central, Hong Kong

Mr. Jack Charlton
162, Tower 1, Grand Central Plaza
138 Shatin Rural Committee Road
Shatin, Hong Kong
November 16th
Account: WI8847367D

Dear Mr. Charlton,

Your Walters International policy has a monthly maintenance charge to cover administration costs. In line with the policy terms and conditions, we review this charge once a year to ensure it remains reasonable in relation to the costs incurred.

As a result of this year's review, the charge will rise from HK$ 86.20 to HK$ 86.90, effective January 1. If you have any questions regarding this charge, please contact your financial adviser.

Yours sincerely,

Norbert Stiles

Norbert Stiles
Pensions Investment Manager
Walters International

9. What is the purpose of the letter?

(A) To introduce a new pension adviser
(B) To offer employment
(C) To announce an increase in charges
(D) To conduct a review

10. In which area does Norbert Stiles work?

(A) Politics
(B) Finance
(C) Publishing
(D) Leisure

11. What is Mr. Charlton advised to do if he has questions about the letter?

(A) Call a pensions investment manager
(B) Check Walters International's homepage
(C) Contact his financial adviser
(D) Send an e-mail to Norbert Stiles

12. What is indicated about Walters International?

(A) They are located in Shatin, Hong Kong.
(B) They review their charges annually.
(C) Their business is rapidly expanding.
(D) They are a leading financial company.

Communicative Training

Part 7 で取り上げた手紙を使ってパートナーと英語で互いに質問をしてみましょう。答える際は、"Yes." や "No." だけで終わらないよう適宜、情報を追加しましょう。

Student A
Student B (パートナー) に下記の質問をしてみましょう。

Student B
Student A (パートナー) の質問に対して Part 7 の英文を見ながら答えましょう。

1. Did Mr. Charlton write the letter?
2. What is Mr. Charlton's account number?
3. Who is Norbert Stiles?
4. How much is Mr. Charlton's current monthly maintenance charge?
5. Will his monthly maintenance charge go up or down from January 1?
6. How much will it be from January?
7. (You choose!)

UNIT 07 Transportation

 Vocabulary

1. 1〜10 の語句の意味として適切なものを a〜j の中から選びましょう。　🎧 1-80

1. familiarize	＿＿＿＿	a.	（会社などが）営業する、稼働する
2. exhibit	＿＿＿＿	b.	展示
3. subway	＿＿＿＿	c.	修理する
4. repair	＿＿＿＿	d.	運賃
5. demand	＿＿＿＿	e.	地下鉄
6. apologize	＿＿＿＿	f.	（情報などが）有益な、参考になる
7. operate	＿＿＿＿	g.	謝罪する
8. as usual	＿＿＿＿	h.	平常どおり、いつものように
9. fare	＿＿＿＿	i.	習熟させる
10. informative	＿＿＿＿	j.	需要

2. 語群の中から適切な日本語訳を選び、派生語の図を完成させましょう。

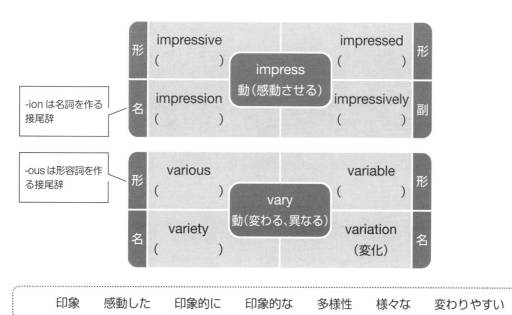

-ion は名詞を作る接尾辞

	impressive ( )		impressed ( )	
形		impress 動（感動させる）		形
名	impression ( )		impressively ( )	副

-ous は形容詞を作る接尾辞

	various ( )		variable ( )	
形		vary 動（変わる、異なる）		形
名	variety ( )		variation （変化）	名

印象　　感動した　　印象的に　　印象的な　　多様性　　様々な　　変わりやすい

Listening Section

Part 1 　解法のコツ　　〈受動態〉

物が中心の写真の場合、その状態を描写するのに受動態が多く使われます。「（物は）〜されている最中だ」という現在進行形の受動態も出題されるので、〈am/is/are+being+過去分詞〉の部分を聞き逃さないようにしましょう。

The motorcycle is parked beside the tree.
（バイクは木のそばに駐車されています）[状態]

The motorcycle is being repaired.
（バイクは修理中です）[動作]

Part 1　**Photographs**　　🎧 1-81, 82

(A) 〜 (D) の英文を聞き、写真を最も適切に描写しているものを選びましょう。

1.

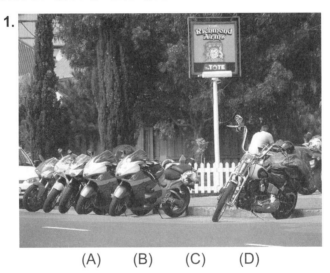

(A)　　(B)　　(C)　　(D)

Part 2　解法のコツ　　〈質問でない疑問文〉

"Why don't you ...?"（〜したらどうですか？）のように、疑問文の形を取っていても、実際には相手に提案したり、依頼したりする表現があります。決まり文句になっているものが多いので慣れておきましょう。

　　問いかけ　　　　Why don't you take a break?
　　正解の応答例　　That's a good idea.

最初に聞こえてくる英文に対する応答として最も適切なものを（A）〜（C）から選びましょう。

2. Mark your answer.　　　　(A)　　　　(B)　　　　(C)
3. Mark your answer.　　　　(A)　　　　(B)　　　　(C)
4. Mark your answer.　　　　(A)　　　　(B)　　　　(C)

Part 3 **解法のコツ**　　〈行動の主体〉

行動の内容を問う設問には、「男性は何をすると言っているか？」のように発話者自身の行動を問う
タイプと、「男性は女性に何をするように言っているか？」のように発話者が相手に依頼する行動を
問うタイプの2つがあります。質問のパターンに慣れておき、どちらの行動が問われているのかが
即座にわかるようにしておきましょう。

・What does the man say he will do?

・What does the man offer to do?

> 問われているのは男性の行動！

・What does the man ask the woman to do?

・What does the man suggest the woman do?

> 問われているのは女性の行動！

Part 3 **Conversations**　　　　　　　　　　　　1-87〜89

会話を聞き、5〜7の設問に対する解答として最も適切なものを（A）〜（D）から選びましょう。

5. Where are the speakers going?

(A) To their office
(B) To the shopping mall
(C) To the airport
(D) To the station

6. What form of transportation will the speakers use?

(A) Bus
(B) Taxi
(C) Train
(D) Subway

7. What does the woman suggest?

(A) Taking the car
(B) Catching a taxi
(C) Staying at home
(D) Leaving immediately

Part 4 　解法のコツ 　〈交通アナウンス〉

交通機関に関するアナウンスには、下記のような基本的な流れがあるので、情報がどのような順序で出てくるか予測することができます。慣れておきましょう。

1. 呼びかけ	Attention, all passengers for Birmingham! ⇒対象は乗客	
2. 目的	The delayed 9:30 train to Birmingham is expected to arrive around 9:50. ⇒電車の到着時間のお知らせ	
3. 追加情報、注意事項	Please note the train will be arriving at Platform 3. ⇒到着ホームのお知らせ	
4. 結び	We apologize for the delay, and thank you for your understanding. ⇒電車の遅延に対するお詫びと謝辞	

Part 4 　Talks 　　　　　　　　　　　 　1-90〜92

トークを聞き、8 〜 10 の設問に対する解答として最も適切なものを（A）〜（D）から選びましょう。

8. Where would you hear this announcement?

(A) At a fire station
(B) At the airport
(C) At a bus station
(D) At a train station

9. What happened at Macclesfield?

(A) A traffic accident
(B) A fire
(C) A train strike
(D) A power failure

10. What are passengers traveling to London asked to do?

(A) Take the 8:42 train
(B) Travel via Macclesfield
(C) Travel via Sheffield
(D) Take the shuttle bus

Communicative Training

1. Part 2 のスクリプトにある最初の問いかけを使ってパートナーと英語で互いに質問をしてみましょう。質問に答える際は、下の回答例を参考にしましょう。なお、スクリプトは教員から配布されます。

Student A
Student B（パートナー）に Part 2 のスクリプトにある最初の問いかけをしてみましょう。

Student B
Student A（パートナー）の質問に対して下の回答例を参考に答えましょう。

Q2	Q3	Q4
・もちろんです。どうぞ乗ってください。 ・すみませんが、できません。 ・すみません。これから家に帰らないといけません。 ・(You choose!)	・ええ、そうしましょう。 ・良い考えですね。 ・バスに乗りませんか？ ・(You choose!)	・もちろんです。はい、どうぞ。 ・いいですよ。少々お待ちください。 ・すみません。私たちは地図を持っていないのです。 ・(You choose!)

2. Part 3 の対話スクリプトの内容について、パートナーと英語で互いに質問をしてみましょう。質問に答える際は、対話スクリプトだけを見るようにし、下の質問は見ないようにしましょう。なお、スクリプトは教員から配布されます。

Student A
Student B（パートナー）に下記の質問をしてみましょう。

Student B
Student A（パートナー）の質問に対して Part 3 の対話スクリプトを見ながら答えましょう。

1. Where are they going?
2. How is the weather?
3. Is the woman willing to drive?
4. Does the man think that they should leave now?
5. (You choose!)

Reading Section

Part 5　**解法のコツ**　〈代名詞問題 1〉

選択肢に代名詞が並んでいる場合は、その代名詞が指す名詞が①単数か複数か？　②人かどうか？　の2点に注意しましょう。また、下の表（一人称の代名詞）を参考にして人称代名詞・所有代名詞・再帰代名詞の働きについても確認しておきましょう。

数	人称代名詞			所有代名詞 ＊「～のもの」という意味を表します。	再帰代名詞 ＊「～自身」という意味を表します。
	主格 ＊主語として使われます。	所有格 ＊「～の」という意味を表します。	目的格 ＊目的語として使われます。		
単数形	I	my	me	mine	myself
複数形	we	our	us	ours	ourselves

☆Check☆

1～4の英文中のカッコ内から正しい語を選び○で囲みましょう。

1. Eric put the document into (its / his / him) bag.
2. I can't find my keys. Where are (them / their / they)?
3. Please call (it / his / us) if you have questions.
4. Lily is a close friend of (my / me / mine).

Part 5　**Incomplete Sentences**

英文を完成させるのに最も適切な語句を（A）～（D）から選びましょう。

1. You need to make ------- own travel arrangements.

(A) you
(B) your
(C) yours
(D) yourself

2. Employees must familiarize ------- with the new safety manual.
(A) themselves
(B) it
(C) their
(D) them

3. We canceled our trip because ------- couldn't get seats on the same flight.
(A) our
(B) us
(C) we
(D) it

4. The city is planning to improve ------- public transportation.
(A) its
(B) they
(C) it
(D) their

文挿入問題は語句挿入問題と比べると難易度が高いため、時間との勝負になる実際の試験では、解答の順序を最後にしたほうが得策です。文章の途中に文挿入問題があると、つい空所の順番に解きたくなりますが、語句挿入問題を優先したほうが良いでしょう。リーディングセクションでは、Part 5 ～ 6 にあまり時間をかけず、大量の英文を読まなければならない Part 7 にできるだけ多くの時間をかけるのが鉄則です。

This amazing interactive trip through the history of public transportation is really enjoyable as well as informative. ----7.---- . The Expo's hours are 10:00 A.M. to 6:00 P.M. daily. Tickets are ----8.---- at the door.

> 実際の試験では、**7** の文挿入問題より **8** の語句挿入問題を先に解きましょう。

Part 6 Text Completion

次の英文を読み、空所に入れるのに最も適切な語句や文を（A）～（D）から選びましょう。

Questions 5-8 refer to the following announcement.

The Transportation Expo

The Transportation Expo is on now at McCormick Place ----5.---- the end of July. This year's theme is the past, present and future of transportation.

There is too much to see and do at the Expo, but you shouldn't ----6.---- the CTA exhibit. This amazing interactive trip through the history of public transportation is really enjoyable as well as informative. ----7.---- .

The Expo's hours are 10:00 A.M. to 6:00 P.M. daily. Tickets are ----8.---- at the door.

---

5. (A) through
(B) at
(C) on
(D) in

6. (A) take
(B) look
(C) see
(D) miss

7. (A) The Transportation Expo started in 2001.
(B) Last year's Expo turned out to be a great success.
(C) It has equal appeal to kids and kids at heart.
(D) McCormick Place is one of the largest convention centers in the U.S.

8. (A) avail
(B) available
(C) availably
(D) availability

工事や店舗開店のお知らせなど、不特定多数の人に向けた告知や案内も Part 7 ではよく出題されます。こうした告知では、記される情報に一定の順番があるので、下の例で確認しておきましょう。問題を先読みし、どんな情報を探すべきかを頭に入れると、文書の中でどのあたりにその情報が書かれているのか見当がつくようになります。

運賃値上げ告知の例

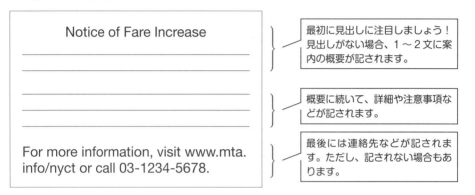

Notice of Fare Increase

For more information, visit www.mta. info/nyct or call 03-1234-5678.

最初に見出しに注目しましょう！見出しがない場合、1～2文に案内の概要が記されます。

概要に続いて、詳細や注意事項などが記されます。

最後には連絡先などが記されます。ただし、記されない場合もあります。

Part 7 / Reading Comprehension

次の英文を読み、設問に対する答えとして最も適切なものを（A）～（D）から選びましょう。

Questions 9-12 refer to the following notice.

Bus Service Changes

★ Metro Bus 201 service
Triffid Park will be closed for road maintenance between West Street and University Drive from January 4 until March 18. Metro Bus 201 service will divert via Greenwood House and Marcus Way.

★ Metro Bus 5 Sunday service
Due to a lack of demand, the Metro Bus 5 Sunday service will be canceled from January 4. This route will continue to operate on weekdays and Saturdays as usual.

★ Route 45 Goodways Coaches to Roughton Estate (from December 10)
Due to vehicles parking too close to the junction of Shaw Drive and Carrick Street, the #45 coach service is unable to access Roughton Estate. Passengers are advised to get off at Maguire Lane.

9. What is the purpose of this notice?

(A) To advertise a special rate
(B) To announce bus schedule changes
(C) To introduce a new vehicle
(D) To explain reasons for the fare raise

10. What will Metro Bus 201 service do from January 4?

(A) Operate only on the weekend
(B) Operate only on weekdays
(C) Resume its normal route
(D) Change its route

11. Why will Metro Bus 5 Sunday service be canceled from January 4?

(A) The road will be closed for maintenance.
(B) The demand remains strong.
(C) Not many people use the service.
(D) Bus drivers are not available.

12. What should passengers do if they want to go to Roughton Estate?

(A) Get off at Maguire Lane
(B) Get off at Shaw Drive
(C) Use Metro Bus 201 service
(D) Use the Metro Bus 5 Sunday service

Communicative Training

Part 7 で取り上げた告知を使ってパートナーと英語で互いに質問をしてみましょう。答える際は、"Yes." や "No." だけで終わらないよう適宜、情報を追加しましょう。

Student A
Student B（パートナー）に下記の質問をしてみましょう。

Student B
Student A（パートナー）の質問に対して Part 7 の英文を見ながら答えましょう。

1. Is this notice about the bus fare?
2. What is this notice about?
3. Why will Triffid Park be closed from January 4 until March 18?
4. Will Metro Bus 201 service change its route from January 4?
5. What will happen to the Metro Bus 5 Sunday service from January 4?
6. Why is the #45 coach service unable to access Roughton Estate?
7. (You choose!)

本テキストで取り上げている接尾辞一覧 3

　接尾辞の中には、語の後ろに付いて動詞や副詞を作るものもあります。例えば origine（起源）という名詞の後ろに -ate がつくことにより originate（始まる）という動詞になります。ただし、-ate という接尾辞は必ずしも動詞とは限らず、形容詞を作る場合もあるので注意が必要です。次の表を使って本テキストで取り上げている動詞、副詞を作る接尾辞を確認しましょう。

動詞を作る接尾辞

接尾辞	意味	例
-ate*	～にする	originate（始まる）（< origin）
-en		widen（～を広くする）（< wide）
-fy, -ify		simplify（単純化する）（< simple）
-ize		specialize（専門にする）（< special）

＊必ずしも動詞とは限らず、fortunate（幸運な）のように形容詞を作る場合もあるので注意が必要。

副詞を作る接尾辞

接尾辞	意味	例
-ly*	～なように	specially（特別に）（< special）

＊必ずしも副詞とは限らず、weekly（毎週の）のように形容詞を作る場合もあるので注意が必要。

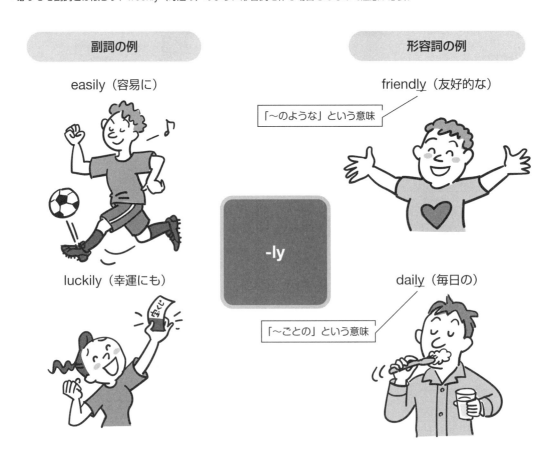

副詞の例

easily（容易に）

luckily（幸運にも）

-ly

形容詞の例

friendly（友好的な）

「～のような」という意味

daily（毎日の）

「～ごとの」という意味

UNIT 08 Technology

 Vocabulary

1. 1 〜 10 の語句の意味として適切なものを a 〜 j の中から選びましょう。 🎧 2-01

1. production	＿＿＿	a. 利益
2. install	＿＿＿	b. 適切な
3. responsible	＿＿＿	c. 保証書
4. admission	＿＿＿	d. 責任がある
5. profit	＿＿＿	e. 確信して
6. defective	＿＿＿	f. 入場
7. warranty	＿＿＿	g. 〜を設置する
8. adequate	＿＿＿	h. 四半期
9. quarter	＿＿＿	i. 欠陥のある
10. confident	＿＿＿	j. 生産

2. 語群の中から適切な日本語訳を選び、派生語の表を完成させましょう。

人を表す名詞を作る 主な接尾辞	もとの単語	人を表す名詞
-or	instruct（　　　　）	instructor（指導者）
-er	examine（試験する）	examiner（　　　）
-ee		examinee（　　　）
-ant	apply（　　　）	applicant（　　　）
-ist	economy（経済）	economist（　　　）
-ian	music（音楽）	musician（　　　）

> 受験者　　経済学者　　応募する　　応募者　　音楽家　　指導する　　試験官

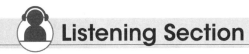

Listening Section

Part 1　解法のコツ　〈現在完了形〉

写真描写問題では、「~している」という現在進行形が中心ですが、「~してしまった」のような現在完了形が使われることもあります。物が中心の写真の場合、「(物は)~されてしまった」という現在完了形の受動態も出題されるので、〈have/has+been+過去分詞〉の部分を聞き逃さないようにしましょう。

☆Check☆

下の写真の描写として最も適切な英文を 1 ~ 4 の中から選びましょう。

1. A man is opening a drawer.
2. A man has opened a drawer.
3. Some drawers are open.
4. A drawer has been left open.

> 人が写っていない写真で、人が主語である文が正解になることはまずありません。

Part 1　**Photographs**　　　　🎧 CD 2-02, 03

(A) ~ (D) の英文を聞き、写真を最も適切に描写しているものを選びましょう。

1.

(A)　　(B)　　(C)　　(D)

Part 2　解法のコツ　〈平叙文〉

最初に聞こえてくる文は疑問文がほとんどですが、中には平叙文もあります。例えば、「このパソコンはどこかおかしい」と伝えることで、解決策や援助を求めるというように、何かを伝えて相手の応答を期待するタイプです。いろんなパターンがありますので、少しずつ慣れましょう。

問いかけ　　　Something is wrong with this computer.
正解の応答例　Why don't you use mine?

最初に聞こえてくる英文に対する応答として最も適切なものを（A）〜（C）から選びましょう。

2. Mark your answer.　　(A)　　(B)　　(C)
3. Mark your answer.　　(A)　　(B)　　(C)
4. Mark your answer.　　(A)　　(B)　　(C)

Part 3　解法のコツ　〈表現の言いかえ〉

正解の選択肢は、会話の中で使われていた表現をそのまま使うのではなく、別の表現で言いかえた形になっていることがよくあります。下の例では、正解の選択肢は、"I'd like you to <u>shut the computer off and then turn it back on</u>." という男性の発言の下線部を restart a computer と言いかえています。選択肢の中に会話で使われていた表現を見つけても、それに飛びつかないようにしましょう。

ex.)

Woman: Can you help me? Something is wrong with my computer. I keep hearing a loud noise.

Man: 　　OK. First, I'd like you to <u>shut the computer off and then turn it back on</u>.

■ What does the man ask the woman to do?

　（A）Restart a computer
　　　　　　　⇒正解は会話内のポイントとなる発言（下線部）を言いかえています！
　（B）Shut down the window
　　　　　　　⇒会話で出てきた表現（shut）はひっかけとして使われています。
　（C）Buy a new computer
　（D）Call the help desk

Part 3 **Conversations**
  2-08〜10

会話を聞き、5〜7の設問に対する解答として最も適切なものを（A）〜（D）から選びましょう。

5. What is wrong with the man's computer?

　（A）It keeps freezing.
　（B）It suddenly restarts itself.
　（C）It keeps sending a warning.
　（D）It makes a strange noise.

6. What does the woman ask the man?

　（A）When he bought his computer
　（B）When the trouble happened
　（C）Whether he called tech support or not
　（D）Whether he saved his file or not

7. What does the man ask the woman to do?

　（A）Fix his computer
　（B）Lend him her computer
　（C）Tell him a phone number
　（D）Memorize the number for tech support

Part 4 　**解法のコツ**　〈留守番電話のメッセージ〉

留守番電話のメッセージには、下記のような基本的な流れがあるので、情報がどのような順序で出てくるか予測することができます。慣れておきましょう。

1. 自己紹介	This is Ted Smith from First Electric. ⇒社名および氏名の連絡
2. 目的	I'm calling to confirm the delivery of your new air conditioner tomorrow morning. ⇒商品配達日のお知らせ
3. 追加情報、注意事項	Our service engineers will arrive sometime between 9 A.M. and 12 noon to install it. ⇒具体的な時間の連絡
4. 依頼事項* *必要な場合のみ	If the time is inconvenient, please call our office at 555-0179. ⇒連絡先の通知

Part 4 　**Talks**　 2-11～13

トークを聞き、8 ～ 10 の設問に対する解答として最も適切なものを（A）～（D）から選びましょう。

8. Why did the speaker make the call?

(A) To cancel an appointment
(B) To make an appointment
(C) To confirm access to the house
(D) To reschedule an installation

9. How long will the whole installation take?

(A) A few hours
(B) About 5 hours
(C) Between 6 and 8 hours
(D) Between 8 and 10 hours

10. What is the listener asked to do?

(A) Pay for the panel on the installment plan
(B) Make an immediate payment
(C) Go out next Wednesday
(D) Return the call

Communicative Training

1. Part 2 のスクリプトにある最初の問いかけを使ってパートナーと英語で互いに質問をしてみましょう。質問に答える際は、下の回答例を参考にしましょう。なお、スクリプトは教員から配布されます。

Student A
Student B（パートナー）に Part 2 のスクリプトにある最初の問いかけをしてみましょう。

Student B
Student A（パートナー）の質問に対して下の回答例を参考に答えましょう。

Q2
・わかりました。私が見てあげましょう。
・何が問題なのですか？
・ケンに助けを頼んだらどうですか？
・（You choose!）

Q3
・はい、そうします。
・どうやって入手するのですか？
・もう試しました。
・（You choose!）

Q4
・それは良かったですね。
・私も買いたいです。
・本当に？ 私も先週新しいテレビを買ったのですよ。
・（You choose!）

---

2. Part 3 の対話スクリプトの内容について、パートナーと英語で互いに質問をしてみましょう。質問に答える際は、対話スクリプトだけを見るようにし、下の質問は見ないようにしましょう。なお、スクリプトは教員から配布されます。

Student A
Student B（パートナー）に下記の質問をしてみましょう。

Student B
Student A（パートナー）の質問に対して Part 3 の対話スクリプトを見ながら答えましょう。

1. What is the man having trouble with?
2. Did he save what he was working on?
3. What does he ask the woman?
4. What will he probably do next?
5. (You choose!)

Reading Section

Part 5　解法のコツ　〈前置詞問題〉

前置詞は名詞・代名詞の前に置かれて、＜前置詞＋（代）名詞＞の形で形容詞や副詞の働きをするので、選択肢に前置詞が並んでいる前置詞問題では、まず空所の直後にある（代）名詞に着目しましょう。また、complain about（～に不満を述べる）や interested in（～に興味を持って）のように、動詞や形容詞とセットになって決まった意味を表す表現も出題されるので、空所の直前にも注意を払いましょう。

Check

1 ～ 4 の英文中のカッコ内から正しい語を選び○で囲みましょう。

1. The package arrived (in / at / on) Wednesday.
2. Let's meet again here (in / at / on) an hour.
3. Some people believe (about / for / in) ghosts.
4. Mike is very proud (of / in / at) his son.

Part 5　Incomplete Sentences

英文を完成させるのに最も適切な語句を（A）～（D）から選びましょう。

1. The new production system will be completed ------- the end of this month.

(A) on
(B) by
(C) until
(D) to

2. Ms. Johnson is responsible ------- designing the entire project.

(A) of
(B) in
(C) to
(D) for

3. Admission to the seminar was limited ------- 100 participants.

(A) for
(B) on
(C) to
(D) at

4. ------- the efforts of the whole team, the project turned out to be a great success.

(A) Thanks to
(B) Instead of
(C) According to
(D) Up to

Unit 4 ～ 5 で 2 つの文をつなぐ主な副詞（句）を確認したので、実際の問題形式で確認してみましょう。結果（したがって）、逆接（しかし）、情報追加（さらに）、例示（例えば）、順序（最初に）のように、パターンが決まっているので、問題演習を繰り返して慣れましょう。

Check

空所に当てはまる語句を語群から選んで、1 ～ 2 の英文を完成させましょう。

1. This room isn't large enough for the meeting. (   ), the air-conditioner isn't working.
2. This scanner is very easy to use. (   ), open the cover, and place the paper like this.

語群

> Instead   Furthermore   First   On the other hand   However

Part 6   Text Completion

次の英文を読み、空所に入れるのに最も適切な語句や文を（A）～（D）から選びましょう。

Questions 5-8 refer to the following article.

Profits are up in the technology sector. Astro, Inc. reports that its profits rose 30% this year. The company attributes this ------- the introduction of a new wireless service. ------- .
5. 6.

Tex Communications reported a second quarter profit of $800,000, ------- to a loss of $300,000 during the same period last year.
7.

Profits for Sun Systems were up just 3% this year. ------- , the company remains confident that its new VR technology will gain popularity.
8.

---

5. (A) for
   (B) to
   (C) with
   (D) in

7. (A) compared
   (B) compare
   (C) comparison
   (D) compares

6. (A) In addition, the service will start in the near future.
   (B) The company accepts the introduction of the service as a failure.
   (C) Despite this, the company began operations three years ago.
   (D) The company hopes to expand its service area further next year.

8. (A) Otherwise
   (B) Moreover
   (C) Nevertheless
   (D) Therefore

スケジュール表や納品書、注文書、返品書といった表や記入用紙などもよく出題されます。これらは、比較的語数が少ないので解きやすいと言えます。また、何の文書かがわかれば内容を推測できるので、タイトルを先に確認しましょう。

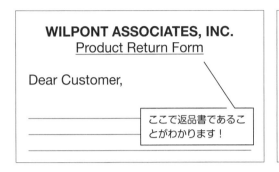

WILPONT ASSOCIATES, INC.
Product Return Form

Dear Customer,

_____

ここで返品書であることがわかります！

WILPONT Fitness Studio
New Member Registration Form

Thank you for your interest in Wilpont Fitness Studio.

_____

ここで入会申込書であることがわかります！

Part 7　Reading Comprehension

次の英文を読み、設問に対する答えとして最も適切なものを（A）～（D）から選びましょう。

Questions 9-12 refer to the following form.

Sanchez Action Figurines [Product return form]

Order No. DM20180823

Why are you returning this? (Check all that apply)

	Accidental order		Unauthorized purchase
	Performance or quality not adequate		Different from Web site description
	Missing parts or accessories		Other (please describe)
✓	Defective / Does not work properly		

Message:

Dear Sir or Madam,

I purchased an Alexis Caganer action figurine online on August 23 this year. However, the product you supplied is defective. It is capable of movement, but the joints are extremely stiff and there is a screw loose in the figurine's head.

Under the terms of the warranty I am mailing to request that you replace the product. Please contact me as soon as possible to let me know how to proceed.

Sincerely,

Dave Moyes

Dmoyes@contractgate.com

9. For whom is the form most likely intended?

(A) Customers who want to answer a questionnaire
(B) Customers who want to return a product
(C) Customers who need help about how to use a product
(D) Customers who lost a product

10. What is wrong with the action figurine?

(A) The size is different.
(B) The color is different.
(C) The joints are too tight.
(D) Some parts are missing.

11. What does Mr. Moyes want?

(A) A refund
(B) A coupon
(C) Missing parts of the product
(D) Replacement of the product

12. The word "terms" in paragraph 2, line 1, is closest in meaning to

(A) periods
(B) prices
(C) conditions
(D) advice

Communicative Training

Part 7 で取り上げた記入用紙を使ってパートナーと英語で互いに質問をしてみましょう。答える際は、"Yes." や "No." だけで終わらないよう適宜、情報を追加しましょう。

Student A
Student B（パートナー）に下記の質問をしてみましょう。

Student B
Student A（パートナー）の質問に対して Part 7 の英文を見ながら答えましょう。

1. What is this form for?
2. What did Mr. Moyes buy on August 23?
3. Why does he want to return the product?
4. What is wrong with the joints of the product?
5. Does he want a refund?
6. Has he returned the product yet?
7. (You choose!)

主な接頭辞一覧

接頭辞とは、unkind の un- など、語の先頭に付けられて、その語の意味あるいは機能を変える要素を指します。例えば、un- は通常、語の意味を逆にしますので、「親切な」という意味の kind に対して unkind は「不親切な」という意味を表します。接尾辞同様、接頭辞の知識があると、未知の単語の意味をある程度推測できます。

接頭辞	意味	例
bi-	2 つの（two）	bimonthly（隔月の）（< monthly）
dis-	～でない（not）	dissatisfied（不満な）（< satisfied）
in-, im-, il-, ir- ※ im- は p や m で始まる形容詞、ir- は r で始まる形容詞、il- は l で始まる形容詞の前につくことが多い。	～でない（not）	incomplete（不完全な）（< complete） impossible（不可能な）（< possible） immature（未熟な）（< mature） illegal（不法の）（< legal） irregular（不規則な）（< regular）
mono-	1 つの（one）	monorail（モノレール）（< rail）
multi-	多くの（many）	multimillion（数百万の）（< million）
non-	～でない（not）	nonprofit（非営利の）（< profit）
post-	後の（after）	postwar（戦後の）（< war）
pre-	前に（before）	prewar（戦前の）（< war）
re-	再び（again）	restart（再出発する）（< start）
semi-	半分（half）	semiautomatic（半自動の）（< automatic）
un-	～でない（not） 元に戻して（back）	uneasy（不安な）（< easy） undo（元に戻す）（< do）

pre- 前に（before）

prewar（戦前の）

post- 後の（after）

postwar（戦後の）

war
戦争

UNIT 09 Health

 Vocabulary

1. 1 ～ 10 の語句の意味として適切なものを a ～ j の中から選びましょう。　2-14

1. agreement	＿＿＿＿	a. 証拠
2. pharmacy	＿＿＿＿	b. 手術
3. prescription	＿＿＿＿	c. 薬局
4. household	＿＿＿＿	d. ウイルス
5. evidence	＿＿＿＿	e. 一家、世帯
6. physical	＿＿＿＿	f. 医療、健康管理
7. operation	＿＿＿＿	g. 集まり、集会
8. virus	＿＿＿＿	h. 処方箋
9. healthcare	＿＿＿＿	i. 身体的な
10. gathering	＿＿＿＿	j. 取り決め、協定

2. 語群の中から適切な日本語訳を選び、派生語の表を完成させましょう。

動詞を作る 接尾辞・接頭辞	もとの単語（名詞・形容詞）	動詞
-en	strength（　　　　　）	strengthen（強くする）
-ate	origin（起源）	originate（　　　　　）
-fy	simple（　　　　　）	simplify（　　　　　）
-ize	apology（　　　　　）	apologize（謝る）
en-	large（大きい）	enlarge（　　　　　）

> 拡大する　　簡単な　　簡単にする　　謝罪　　強さ　　始まる

Listening Section

複数の人物が写っている写真の場合、選択肢の主語がすべて異なる場合があります。それぞれの主語を聞き漏らさないよう、冒頭の主語に注意を払いましょう。

Check

下の写真の描写として最も適切な英文を 1 ～ 4 の中から選びましょう。

1. The baby is lying on the bed.
2. The man is holding a baby in his arms.
3. The woman is sitting up in bed.
4. The couple are watching their baby.

Part 1 　Photographs 　　　　　　　　　　　CD 2-15, 16

(A) ～ (D) の英文を聞き、写真を最も適切に描写しているものを選びましょう。

1.

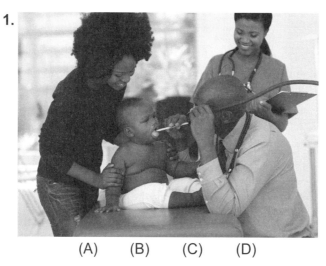

(A)　　(B)　　(C)　　(D)

Part 2 　解法のコツ　〈発音の似た単語〉

最初の問いかけに出てきた単語が含まれた選択肢は不正解である場合がほとんどですが、発音が似た単語や同じ発音で意味の異なる単語が入った選択肢も、多くの場合不正解です。

問いかけ	Would you like to meet my sister?
不正解の応答例	She likes everything neat and tidy.
不正解の応答例	She doesn't eat meat.
正解の応答例	Sure. Why not?

Part 2 / Question-Response

最初に聞こえてくる英文に対する応答として最も適切なものを（A）～（C）から選びましょう。

2. Mark your answer.   (A)   (B)   (C)
3. Mark your answer.   (A)   (B)   (C)
4. Mark your answer.   (A)   (B)   (C)

Part 3 / 解法のコツ　〈話題を問う設問〉

会話の話題を問う設問では、"What is the conversation mainly about?" や "What are the speakers discussing?" のように、何について話しているかをストレートに問うものが中心となります。しかし、この他にも "What is the problem?" や "What is wrong with the car?" のように、話題となっている問題点を具体的に問う形式もありますので慣れておきましょう。

- ・What is the conversation mainly about?　　　　「何についての会話か？」
- ・What are the speakers discussing?
- ・What is wrong with the car?　　　　「（話題となっている）問題点は何か？」
- ・According to the man, what is the problem?

according to で「〜によれば」という意味

Part 3 / Conversations

会話を聞き、5～7の設問に対する解答として最も適切なものを（A）～（D）から選びましょう。

5. What is the conversation mainly about?

- (A) Checkup results
- (B) An operation
- (C) A medical checkup
- (D) A dentist's appointment

6. What does the woman ask the man?

- (A) His preferred day
- (B) When he got a chest X-ray
- (C) His medical history
- (D) His blood type

7. When would be convenient for the man?

- (A) 9 A.M. on Tuesday
- (B) Later than 10 A.M. on Tuesday
- (C) 10 A.M. on Thursday
- (D) Later than 10 A.M. on Thursday

天災への対処など、公共性のある情報を告知する公共放送には、下記のような基本的な流れがあります。情報がどのような順序で出てくるか予測することができるので、慣れておきましょう。

1. 挨拶	This is a public health announcement.
2. 状況	There has been a sharp increase in cases of the new virus.
3. 行動依頼	We must remind you to follow the following three guidelines.
4. 結び	Thank you for your attention.

Part 4　Talks

 2-24〜26

トークを聞き、8 〜 10 の設問に対する解答として最も適切なものを（A）〜（D）から選びましょう。

8. What is this announcement about?

(A) The number of infected people
(B) Public health guidelines
(C) A new healthcare system
(D) How to sanitize your hands

9. What does the speaker say we are faced with?

(A) The possibility of lockdown
(B) The prospect of an economic slowdown
(C) The arrival of a new virus
(D) The collapse of the healthcare system

10. What is the first guideline?

(A) Wash your hands regularly.
(B) Sanitize your hands regularly.
(C) Avoid large gatherings and crowded spaces.
(D) Wear a mask when you go out.

Communicative Training

1. Part 2 のスクリプトにある最初の問いかけを使ってパートナーと英語で互いに質問をして
   みましょう。質問に答える際は、下の回答例を参考にしましょう。なお、スクリプトは教
   員から配布されます。

Student A
Student B（パート
ナー）に Part 2 の
スクリプトにある最
初の問いかけをして
みましょう。

Student B
Student A（パート
ナー）の質問に対し
て下の回答例を参考
に答えましょう。

Q2	Q3	Q4
・頭痛がします。	・病院に行くべきです。	・はい、そうします。
・喉が痛いです。	・薬は飲みましたか？	・わかりました。ありがと
・鼻水が出ます。	・それはいけませんね。	うございます。
・（You choose!）	・（You choose!）	・今飲んでも良いですか？
		・（You choose!）

2. Part 3 の対話スクリプトの内容について、パートナーと英語で互いに質問をしてみましょ
   う。質問に答える際は、対話スクリプトだけを見るようにし、下の質問は見ないようにし
   ましょう。なお、スクリプトは教員から配布されます。

Student A
Student B（パート
ナー）に下記の質問
をしてみましょう。

Student B
Student A（パート
ナー）の質問に対し
て Part 3 の対話ス
クリプトを見ながら
答えましょう。

1. What does the man make an appointment for?
2. Who most likely is the woman?
3. Is Tuesday at 10 A.M. convenient for the man?
4. What does he have at 9 A.M. on Tuesday?
5. （You choose!）

Reading Section

Part 5 　解法のコツ　　〈接続詞問題〉

接続詞問題の場合、空所前後の単語に着目するのではなく、文全体を読んで内容を理解したうえで解くようにしたほうが良いでしょう。また、while と during など、意味の似通った前置詞との区別が問題になることもあり、その場合は接続詞と前置詞が選択肢に混ざった形になります。なお、接続詞と前置詞を見分けるポイントは次のとおりです。

接続詞	その後に主語と動詞を含む語句（＝**節**）が続きます。 ex.) Chuck canceled his trip **because** he was ill.
前置詞	その後に主語と動詞を含まない語句（＝**句**）が続きます。 ex.) Chuck canceled his trip **because of** his illness.

☆Check☆

下線部に注意しながら、1〜4の英文中のカッコ内から正しい語句を選び○で囲みましょう。

1. The hospital is <u>large</u> (and / but) <u>in a good location</u>.

2. Emma arrived (while / during) <u>we were having dinner</u>.

3. Tim can't travel far (because / because of) <u>his state of health</u>.

4. (Although / Despite) <u>I was sick</u>, I had to work overtime.

Part 5 　Incomplete Sentences

英文を完成させるのに最も適切な語句を（A）〜（D）から選びましょう。

1. Computers are useful, ------- they may also cause various health problems.

(A) and
(B) so
(C) because
(D) but

2. Three people were taken to hospital ------- a crash on the expressway.

(A) because
(B) behind
(C) after
(D) while

3. ------- this new diet, I've lost a lot of weight.

(A) Thanks to
(B) According to
(C) In case
(D) Until

4. Health is important. ------- you have your health, nothing else matters.

(A) During
(B) As long as
(C) Although
(D) Despite

2つの文をつなぐ主な副詞（句）については、これまで取り上げたもの以外に、「その一方で」や「それに対して」のように「対比」を表すものもあります。実際の問題形式で確認してみましょう。

☀Check☀

空所に当てはまる語句を語群から選んで、1〜2の英文を完成させましょう。ただし、文の始めにくる単語も小文字にしてあります。

1. My wife only likes classical music. I, (　　　　), like all kinds.
2. It's extremely expensive to live in New York. (　　　　), I pay $2,000 for a one-bedroom apartment.

語群

> finally　　on the other hand　　in addition　　for example

Part 6　Text Completion

次の英文を読み、空所に入れるのに最も適切な語句や文を（A）〜（D）から選びましょう。

Questions 5-8 refer to the following article.

Just Aid ranks ----5.---- the best online pharmacies in the U.S.A. They sell prescription and over-the-counter medicines to customers at very ----6.--- rates, thanks to their agreements with medical companies.

Just Aid also ----7.---- beauty products, household requirements, baby care products, and lots more. It is one of the top online shopping Web sites in the U.S. ----8.---- .

---

5. (A) as
(B) on
(C) at
(D) among

6. (A) afford
(B) afforded
(C) affordable
(D) affordably

7. (A) supplied
(B) supplying
(C) will supply
(D) supplies

8. (A) However, they also sell prescription glasses.
(B) In fact, it ranked highest for customer satisfaction in J.D. Power's 2021 study.
(C) Therefore, they stopped selling online.
(D) As a result, Just Aid also runs an online pharmacy.

新聞や雑誌に掲載された記事は、語数が多く、語彙も難しい傾向にあります。ただし、第1段落目に全体の要旨がまとめてあるので、次のような概要に関する問題は第1段落をしっかり読めば解くことができます。諦めないようにしましょう。

- What does the article mainly discuss?
- What is the purpose of the article?
- What is the article about?

いずれも記事の概要を尋ねる設問です。

記事の例

Too Much Coffee

September 15— _____

_____

_____

_____

第1段落に全体の要旨がまとめてあります。最初に日付が書かれていることもあります。

Part 7　Reading Comprehension

次の英文を読み、設問に対する答えとして最も適切なものを（A）〜（D）から選びましょう。

Questions 9-12 refer to the following article.

Promoting Physical Activity in Our Community

Nothing is more important in life than our good health, and there's abundant scientific evidence that regular physical activity is one of the key contributors to our overall health and well-being. — [1] —. Regardless of gender, age, occupation, ethnicity or race, following a more active lifestyle—one that promotes bodily movement—provides enormous benefits. — [2] —. Even if you're suffering from a chronic disease or disability, light but regular physical activity will help to improve your strength, immunity and general conditioning.

— [3] —. Remember, it's never too late to change your lifestyle and improve your health. We can offer personal training consultations and programs. — [4] —.

9. What does the article mainly discuss?

  (A) The importance of scientific evidence

  (B) The health hazards that exercise causes

  (C) The value of physical activity

  (D) How to become a community adviser

10. The word "chronic" in paragraph 1, line 6, is closest in meaning to

  (A) long-term

  (B) acute

  (C) occasional

  (D) temporary

11. In which of the positions marked [1], [2], [3], and [4] does the following sentence best belong?
"Just pick up the phone and talk to one of our community advisers."

  (A) [1]

  (B) [2]

  (C) [3]

  (D) [4]

12. What does the article recommend that the readers do?

  (A) Call an adviser in their community

  (B) Offer personal training consultations

  (C) Lose weight

  (D) Register as a community adviser

Communicative Training

Part 7 で取り上げた記事を使ってパートナーと英語で互いに質問をしてみましょう。答える際は、"Yes." や "No." だけで終わらないよう適宜、情報を追加しましょう。

Student A
Student B（パートナー）に下記の質問をしてみましょう。

Student B
Student A（パートナー）の質問に対して Part 7 の英文を見ながら答えましょう。

1. What is this article about?
2. Is there anything else that is more important than our good health?
3. What is one of the key contributors to our overall health and well-being?
4. If you're suffering from a chronic disease, what kind of physical activity would be helpful?
5. What can they offer to change our lifestyle and improve our health?
6. Do you think you follow an active lifestyle?
7. (You choose!)

本テキストで取り上げているつなぎ言葉一覧

Part 6 の空所補充問題では、単に語彙や文法の知識だけでなく、文脈の理解が必要となる問題も登場します。その場合、「しかし」や「したがって」のように、2 つの文をつなぐ副詞（句）の理解が重要になります。次の表を使って本テキストで取り上げているつなぎ言葉を確認しましょう。

意味	つなぎ言葉
結果（したがって、そのため）	as a result（その結果） therefore（それゆえ） thus（したがって）
逆接（しかし、ところが）	however（しかしながら） nevertheless（それにもかかわらず）
情報追加（さらに、しかも）	furthermore（その上） in addition（その上） moreover（さらに）
例示（例えば）	for example（例えば） for instance（例えば）
順序（まず、それから、最後に）	first（最初に） next（次に） then（それから） finally（最後に）
条件（さもなければ）	otherwise（さもなければ）
対比（それに対して）	on the other hand（一方で）

First, ...
Next, ...
Then, ...
Finally, ...

UNIT 10 Travel

Vocabulary

1. 1 〜 10 の語句の意味として適切なものを a 〜 j の中から選びましょう。　🔊 2-27

1. reserve	_____	a. 搭乗券
2. luxurious	_____	b. 結果、成果
3. direct flight	_____	c. 豪華な
4. fluency	_____	d. 流暢さ
5. résumé	_____	e. 〜を同封する
6. hesitate	_____	f. 直行便
7. outcome	_____	g. 履歴書
8. situation	_____	h. 状況
9. boarding pass	_____	i. 予約する
10. enclose	_____	j. ためらう

2. 語群の中から適切な日本語訳を選び、派生語の表を完成させましょう。

形容詞を作る主な接尾辞	もとの単語（名詞・動詞）	形容詞
-ive	act（　　　　　）	active（活動的な）
-ent	urge 動（強く勧める）名（衝動）	urgent（　　　　　）
-ful	forget（忘れる）	forgetful（　　　　）
-less	fear 動（　　　　）名（恐れ）	fearless（　　　　）
-al	origin（起源）	original（　　　　）
-ous	fame（　　　　）	famous（有名な）
-able	value（価値）	valuable（　　　　）

> 恐れる　忘れっぽい　価値がある　名声　緊急の　独創的な　恐れを知らない　行動する

Part 1 解法のコツ 〈先入観の排除〉

写真の中で大きく写っている物にはどうしても注意が向きがちですが、必ずしもそれを描写する文が正解とは限りません。先入観を持たずにすべての文を聞いてから解答しましょう。また、写真に人が写っていても、人が主語となる文が正解とは限らない点も要注意です。

☆Check☆

下の写真の描写として最も適切な英文を 1 〜 4 の中から選びましょう。

1. The man is pulling his suitcase behind him.
2. Two airplanes are flying high in the sky.
3. The chairs are unoccupied.
4. The man is on a plane.

Part 1 Photographs 🎧 2-28, 29

（A）〜（D）の英文を聞き、写真を最も適切に描写しているものを選びましょう。

1.

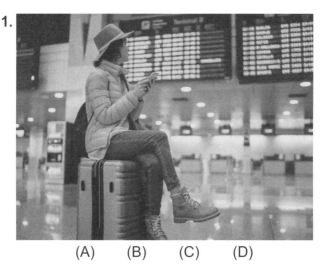

(A)　　(B)　　(C)　　(D)

Part 2 解法のコツ 〈同一単語の繰り返し 2〉

最初の問いかけに出てきた単語や発音の似た単語が入った選択肢は不正解である場合がほとんどですが、A or B という形式の選択疑問文は例外です。同じ単語が入った選択肢が正解となる場合もあるので注意しましょう。

問いかけ　　Do you have time to discuss next year's budget today or tomorrow?
正解の応答例　I can discuss it today.

最初に聞こえてくる英文に対する応答として最も適切なものを（A）〜（C）から選びましょう。

2. Mark your answer. 　(A)　　(B)　　(C)
3. Mark your answer. 　(A)　　(B)　　(C)
4. Mark your answer. 　(A)　　(B)　　(C)

Part 3 解法のコツ 　〈理由を問う設問〉

理由を尋ねる設問では、"Why did the man arrive late?" のように why で始まるものが定番です。会話の中の発言を取り上げ、その発言をした理由を問うタイプもあるので慣れておきましょう。また、選択肢は "He was sick." のように文タイプか、"To open a bank account" のような不定詞のタイプとなります。不定詞タイプの選択肢は短いものが多いので、できるだけ会話を聞く前に選択肢まで見ておくようにしましょう。会話のヒントが得られます。

■ Why does the man say, "But I've got a call from a client in 10 minutes"?

　(A) To share good news
　(B) To request some help
　(C) To cancel a meeting
　(D) To end the conversation

不定詞タイプの選択肢は短いものが多い！

会話の中に出てくる発言です。

Part 3 **Conversations** 2-34〜36

会話を聞き、5 〜 7 の設問に対する解答として最も適切なものを（A）〜（D）から選びましょう。

5. Who most likely is the man?

　(A) A tour guide
　(B) A hotel receptionist
　(C) A travel agent
　(D) A flight attendant

6. Why is the woman calling?

　(A) To book a hotel room
　(B) To change a flight reservation
　(C) To ask about a lost item
　(D) To request a refund

7. What does the man say he needs to do?

　(A) Check with his boss
　(B) Make sure that seats are available
　(C) Call the Shanghai office
　(D) Fill out a form

Part 3 同様に、Part 4 でも図表付きの問題が出題されます。3 つの設問のうち図表に関するものは 1 つで、"Look at the graphic." という指示が設問の冒頭に書かれています。トークを聞く前に、図表を見て何が書いてあるのか確認しておきましょう。

> ハイキングコースの地図だとわかります！

10. Look at the graphic. Which route does the speaker plan on taking?
    (A) Route A
    (B) Route B
    (C) Route C
    (D) Route D

Part 4   **Talks**

 2-37〜39

トークを聞き、8 〜 10 の設問に対する解答として最も適切なものを（A）〜（D）から選びましょう。

8. Who is this talk directed to?
   (A) Passengers
   (B) Hikers
   (C) Tour guides
   (D) Volunteers

9. What happened near Della Falls?
   (A) A traffic accident
   (B) A flood
   (C) A fire
   (D) A landslide

10. Look at the graphic. Which route does the speaker plan on taking?
    (A) Route A
    (B) Route B
    (C) Route C
    (D) Route D

Communicative Training

1. Part 2 のスクリプトにある最初の問いかけを使ってパートナーと英語で互いに質問をしてみましょう。質問に答える際は、下の回答例を参考にしましょう。なお、スクリプトは教員から配布されます。

Student A
Student B（パートナー）に Part 2 のスクリプトにある最初の問いかけをしてみましょう。

Student B
Student A（パートナー）の質問に対して下の回答例を参考に答えましょう。

Q2
・電車のほうがより簡単です。
・バスのほうが簡単ですが、時間がよりかかります。
・すみません、よくわかりません。
・（You choose!）

Q3
・ええ、良いですよ。
・すみません、今は忙しいです。
・すみません、他の人に頼んでもらえませんか？
・（You choose!）

Q4
・自分でします。
・（私のために）予約してもらえますか？
・すでに自分で（予約）しました。
・（You choose!）

2. Part 3 の対話スクリプトの内容について、パートナーと英語で互いに質問をしてみましょう。質問に答える際は、対話スクリプトだけを見るようにし、下の質問は見ないようにしましょう。なお、スクリプトは教員から配布されます。

Student A
Student B（パートナー）に下記の質問をしてみましょう。

Student B
Student A（パートナー）の質問に対して Part 3 の対話スクリプトを見ながら答えましょう。

1. What is the last name of the woman?
2. Has the man given the tickets to her yet?
3. Does she want to change to the earlier flight or the later one?
4. What does she say about the later flight?
5. (You choose!)

Reading Section

動詞の形を問う問題で選択肢に ing 形があった場合、現在分詞と動名詞の 2 つの可能性があるので注意しましょう。動名詞は、「～すること」のように動詞を名詞化するものですが、動詞が名詞の働きをするものには to 不定詞もあるので、この 2 つの使い分けにも慣れておく必要があります。

Check

1 ～ 4 の英文中のカッコ内から正しい語句を選び○で囲みましょう。

1. (Walking / Walk) at night is dangerous in this area.
2. Mr. Reynolds is (traveled / traveling) abroad.
3. We're considering (to take / taking) a trip around the world.
4. I hope (to visit / visiting) Spain someday.

Part 5   Incomplete Sentences

英文を完成させるのに最も適切な語句を（A）～（D）から選びましょう。

1. ------- airline tickets online saves a lot of time and money.

(A) Reserving
(B) Reserve
(C) Reserves
(D) Reserved

2. Our travel agent advised us ------- this luxurious new hotel.

(A) try
(B) trying
(C) to try
(D) tried

3. I suggest ------- a direct flight instead of a connecting flight.

(A) took
(B) to take
(C) taken
(D) taking

4. Ted seems very busy ------- ready for his overseas travel next week.

(A) get
(B) getting
(C) to get
(D) got

求人案内などを扱った英文では、「仕事内容には～が含まれます」や「応募者には～が必要です」のような定型表現が数多く登場します。こうした定型表現が語句挿入問題や文挿入問題に使われることもあるので、ぜひ慣れておきましょう。

Check

1～4の英文中で下線を引いた語句とその日本語訳とを線で結びましょう。

1. Please <u>send your résumé</u> to Kate Ross.　　　•　　　• 職務には～が含まれます
2. <u>Applicants must have</u> a university degree in tourism. •　　　• 応募者には～が必要です
3. <u>Duties include</u> frequent visits to clients.　　　•　　　• ～の経歴がある
4. We are looking for someone <u>with a background in</u> marketing.　　　•　　　• 履歴書を送る

Part 6　Text Completion

次の英文を読み、空所に入れるのに最も適切な語句や文を（A）～（D）から選びましょう。

Questions 5-8 refer to the following advertisement.

Discovery Tours Ltd., one of Canada's leading tour companies, is currently seeking an ---5--- guide to lead our tours in South America.

Applicants must have at least three years of experience in the tourist industry, ---6--- excellent communication skills. Fluency in Spanish is preferred, but not essential.

---7--- for the position, please send your résumé to Kate Ross, the personnel director, at kateross@discoverytours.com. ---8--- . Applications received after this deadline will not be read.

5. (A) experience
(B) experienced
(C) experiencing
(D) experiences

6. (A) except
(B) in regard to
(C) as for
(D) as well as

7. (A) To apply
(B) Applying
(C) Apply
(D) Applied

8. (A) If you enjoy traveling, this is the job for you.
(B) We are interested in applicants with foreign language skills.
(C) Applications must be submitted by June 10 at the latest.
(D) We will contact qualified candidates after we review the applications.

Part 7 の後半では、複数の文書が 1 セットになった問題が計 5 題出題されます。その内訳は次のようになっています。

名称	形式	出題数
ダブルパッセージ問題	2 つの文書を読み 5 つの設問に答える	2 題
トリプルパッセージ問題	3 つの文書を読み 5 つの設問に答える	3 題

問題の指示文は次のようになっており、文書の形式がわかります。

Questions 176-180 refer to the following e-mail and schedule.
　　　　⇒ダブルパッセージ問題の例

Questions 196-200 refer to the following Web page and e-mails.
　　　　⇒トリプルパッセージ問題の例

いずれも難易度が高く、5 つの設問の中には必ず複数の文書の情報を組み合わせないと解けない問題が含まれています。ただし、それ以外の問題はシングルパッセージ問題と変わらないので、そうした問題から先に取り組むと良いでしょう。複数の文書の中で特定の文書に関する設問には、According to the form（その用紙によれば）のような指示が含まれることもあります。

11. According to the form, why should a customer contact Mr. Smith?

複数文書のうち、the form だけを読めば解ける問題です。

Part 7　Reading Comprehension

次の英文を読み、設問に対する答えとして最も適切なものを（A）～（D）から選びましょう。

Questions 9-13 refer to the following letter and e-mail.

November 2

Customer Services
Ostiana Air (Seoul Office)
Level 42, Gangnam Commerce Center,
123 Nonhyeon-ro, Gangnam-gu,
Seoul 06236, Korea

Dear Sir or Madam,

As requested, please find enclosed the boarding pass stub of my recent Ostiana Air flight from Almaty. The air miles have not yet been credited, and although I tried to input the data to your online service, it failed each time (and received a "Code Z99" response).

My membership number is 207653456. My flight OS695 departed Almaty on September 17. My seat number was 23A, Economy class. I trust you will be able to remedy the situation at your earliest possible convenience.

Please do not hesitate to contact me at emiliaharter@gmail.com if you need any further information.

Many thanks,

Emilia Harter

To:	Emilia Harter
From:	Julia Park
Date:	November 10
Subject:	Re: Missing air miles claim

Dear Ms. Harter,

Thank you for your letter dated November 2. I have investigated your claim for missing air miles. However, I regret to inform you that, as you used a discount fare ticket (fare class N), it is not eligible for a mileage award.

I am sorry to be unable to offer you a positive outcome on this occasion, but I hope you will continue to fly Ostiana Air. We look forward to welcoming you on board.

Sincerely,

Julia Park
Customer Services (Golden Miles Program)
Ostiana Air

9. Why was the letter written?

(A) To report a problem
(B) To complete a survey
(C) To offer a positive outcome
(D) To reserve a flight

10. What did Ms. Harter send to Ostiana Air?

(A) A letter only
(B) A letter and a copy of "Code Z99" response
(C) A letter and her boarding pass stub
(D) A letter and a copy of her membership card

11. What most likely is Code Z99?

(A) A flight number
(B) A password
(C) A boarding pass
(D) An error message

12. According to the e-mail, what is stated about Ms. Park?

(A) She regrets having made a mistake.
(B) She examined Ms. Harter's claim.
(C) She issued a new ticket for Ms. Harter.
(D) She offered Ms. Harter a positive outcome.

13. When was the flight that Ms. Park referred to?

(A) September 17
(B) September 23
(C) November 2
(D) November 10

Communicative Training

Part 7 で取り上げた手紙と e メールを使ってパートナーと英語で互いに質問をしてみましょう。答える際は、"Yes." や "No." だけで終わらないよう適宜、情報を追加しましょう。

Student A
Student B（パートナー）に下記の質問をしてみましょう。

Student B
Student A（パートナー）の質問に対して Part 7 の英文を見ながら答えましょう。

1. Who did Ms. Harter send the letter to?
2. Why did she send the letter?
3. Did she send anything with the letter?
4. When did she use OS695?
5. Who replied to the letter from Ms. Harter?
6. Is Ms. Harter's flight eligible for a mileage award with Ostiana Air?
7. (You choose!)

Business

 ## Vocabulary

1. 1 ～ 10 の語句の意味として適切なものを a ～ j の中から選びましょう。　🎧 2-40

1. inquiry	＿＿＿＿	a. 聴衆
2. expertise	＿＿＿＿	b. 見込みがある
3. flyer	＿＿＿＿	c. 議題
4. audience	＿＿＿＿	d. 問い合わせ
5. agenda	＿＿＿＿	e. ～を分ける
6. accommodate	＿＿＿＿	f. チラシ
7. merchandise	＿＿＿＿	g. （人）を収容できる
8. deposit	＿＿＿＿	h. 専門知識
9. divide	＿＿＿＿	i. 頭金、手付金
10. potential	＿＿＿＿	j. 商品

2. 語群の中から適切な日本語訳を選び、派生語の表を完成させましょう。

名詞を作る 主な接尾辞	もとの単語（動詞・形容詞）	名詞
-ence	exist（存在する）	existence （　　　　）
-ness	polite （　　　　）	politeness（礼儀正しさ）
-ion, -sion, -tion	invent（発明する）	invention （　　　）
-ment	equip（備え付ける）	equipment （　　　）
-ity, -ty	secure 動（　　　）形（　　　）	security（安全）

> 安全な　設備　存在　発明（品）　礼儀正しい　～を確保する

Listening Section

Part 1 解法のコツ 〈人物（3人以上）の描写2〉

3人以上の人物が写っている写真の場合、全員の共通点を描写するものが多いですが、特定の人物の動作や服装、持ち物などの描写が正解となる場合もあります。

ᗡCheckᗞ

下の写真の描写として最も適切な英文を1〜4の中から選びましょう。

1. They're writing something.
2. They're all wearing suits.
3. A woman is talking to a group of people.
4. A woman is handing out flyers.

Part 1 **Photographs** 2-41, 42

(A) 〜 (D) の英文を聞き、写真を最も適切に描写しているものを選びましょう。

1.

(A) (B) (C) (D)

Part 2 解法のコツ 〈間接疑問文〉

"Do you know <u>where he lives</u>?" のように、疑問文を平叙文の語順にして目的語や補語として使うタイプ（間接疑問文）では、途中に出てくる疑問詞が聞き取りのポイントになります。聞き逃さないようにしましょう。

問いかけ	Do you know whose keys these are?
不正解の応答例	I left them on your desk.
正解の応答例	I think they're Jason's.

最初に聞こえてくる英文に対する応答として最も適切なものを（A）～（C）から選びましょう。

2. Mark your answer.　　（A）　　　（B）　　　（C）
3. Mark your answer.　　（A）　　　（B）　　　（C）
4. Mark your answer.　　（A）　　　（B）　　　（C）

Part 3 / 解法のコツ　　〈場所を問う設問〉

場所に関する設問は会話が行われている場所に関するものが中心ですが、"Where did the man leave his phone?" のように話題に関するものが出題されることもあります。いずれの場合も、選択肢は場所の名前で短いものが多いので、できるだけ会話を聞く前に選択肢まで見ておくようにしましょう。会話のヒントが得られます。

- Where most likely are the speakers?
- Where is the conversation taking place?
- Where does the conversation take place?

> いずれも会話の行われている場所を尋ねる設問です。

　（A）At a dry cleaner
　（B）At a grocery store
　（C）At a school
　（D）At a hospital

> 短い選択肢が多いのでできれば事前に目を通しましょう。

Part 3 / **Conversations** 2-47～49

会話を聞き、5～7の設問に対する解答として最も適切なものを（A）～（D）から選びましょう。

5. What are the speakers discussing?

　（A）Their budget
　（B）Their meeting
　（C）Their trip
　（D）Their office

6. What does the woman suggest?

　（A）They should meet the next day.
　（B）They should go to the airport.
　（C）The man should cancel his trip.
　（D）She would visit the man's office.

7. Where will they most likely meet the next day?

　（A）In the cafeteria
　（B）In Barry's office
　（C）In the woman's office
　（D）In the man's office

Part 4 　解法のコツ 　〈図表問題 2〉

図表付きの問題では、トークを聞く前に図表を見て何が書いてあるのか確認しておきましょう。特に、人名の記載がある場合はトークの中で触れられることが多いので、必ず目を通しておきましょう。

会議の「議題」が書かれている文書だとわかります。

Agenda
Monthly Staff Meeting

1. Sales report by Adam Baker
2. Budget review by Emily Thompson
3. Professional development by Josh Tucker
4. New personnel system by Luke Pritchett

人名はトークに出る可能性が高いので要チェック！

9. Look at the graphic. What was not discussed at the meeting?
   (A) The sales report
   (B) The budget review
   (C) Professional development
   (D) The new personnel system

Part 4 　Talks

 2-50～52

トークを聞き、8 ～ 10 の設問に対する解答として最も適切なものを（A）～（D）から選びましょう。

Agenda
Monthly Staff Meeting

1. Sales report by Adam Baker
2. Budget review by Emily Thompson
3. Professional development by Josh Tucker
4. New personnel system by Luke Pritchett

8. What was the budget review about?

   (A) Salaries
   (B) Advertising and promotion
   (C) Research and development
   (D) A training seminar

9. Look at the graphic. What was not discussed at the meeting?

   (A) The sales report
   (B) The budget review
   (C) Professional development
   (D) The new personnel system

10. What will the speaker probably do early next week?

   (A) Hold another monthly meeting
   (B) Tell Carol about the meeting in detail
   (C) Review next year's budget
   (D) Take a training seminar

Communicative Training

1. Part 2 のスクリプトにある最初の問いかけを使ってパートナーと英語で互いに質問をしてみましょう。質問に答える際は、下の回答例を参考にしましょう。なお、スクリプトは教員から配布されます。

Student A
Student B（パートナー）に Part 2 のスクリプトにある最初の問いかけをしてみましょう。

Student B
Student A（パートナー）の質問に対して下の回答例を参考に答えましょう。

Q2
・2 階の会議室です。
・わかりません。
・リンダに聞いてもらえませんか？ 彼女が知っているはずです。
・（You choose!）

Q3
・（彼は）3 時には戻ります。
・彼は（それについて）何も言いませんでした。
・わかりません。
・（You choose!）

Q4
・ええ。もう帰って良いですよ。
・どうしたのですか？
・申し訳ないですが、ダメです。
・（You choose!）

2. Part 4 のスクリプトの内容について、パートナーと英語で互いに質問をしてみましょう。質問に答える際は、対話スクリプトだけを見るようにし、下の質問は見ないようにしましょう。なお、スクリプトは教員から配布されます。

Student A
Student B（パートナー）に下記の質問をしてみましょう。

Student B
Student A（パートナー）の質問に対して Part 4 のスクリプトを見ながら答えましょう。

1. Who is calling, Carol or Emily?
2. How did the meeting go?
3. What does the woman say the problem was?
4. What will Adam do at the next meeting?
5. (You choose!)

Reading Section

通常、語彙問題の選択肢は 1 語ですが、次の例のように 2 語以上の場合もあります。

> I'd like to (clear up / break down / check in / take off) any misunderstandings about the matter.

この場合、＜動詞＋前置詞・副詞＞で特別な意味を持つ句動詞の知識が問われています。上記の問題の場合、「（疑問・問題など）を解決する」という意味を持つ clear up が正解になります。語彙学習の際には、こうした句動詞にも目を向けましょう。

⋮Check⋮

1 〜 4 の英文中で下線を引いた語句とその日本語訳とを線で結びましょう。

1. We arranged to meet at six, but she never <u>turned up</u>. •　•〜の電源を入れた
2. Ted asked her to marry him but she <u>turned</u> him <u>down</u>. •　•現れた
3. Maria <u>turned on</u> the air conditioner. •　•〜を提出した
4. Brian <u>turned in</u> the report to his boss. •　•〜を断った

Part 5 Incomplete Sentences

英文を完成させるのに最も適切な語句を（A）〜（D）から選びましょう。

1. Don't forget to ------- your computer when you leave the office.

(A) break out
(B) give out
(C) turn in
(D) turn off

2. Currently, we are ------- a larger office space.

(A) running into
(B) looking for
(C) putting on
(D) taking off

3. Mr. White will ------- this project while the manager is on vacation.

(A) take over
(B) turn in
(C) get off
(D) put on

4. We decided to ------- today's meeting because several key people could not come.

(A) call up
(B) take up
(C) put off
(D) turn off

手紙やeメールでは、「よろしくお願いいたします」や「お返事をいただければ幸いです」のような定型表現が数多く登場します。こうした定型表現に慣れておくと、素早く長文を読むことができるようになるので、ぜひ慣れておきましょう。

Check

1～4の英文中で下線を引いた語句とその日本語訳とを線で結びましょう。

1. <u>Please find attached</u> the schedule for
   the seminar.　　　　　　　　　　　　・　　　・お問い合わせありがとうございます
2. I <u>look forward to hearing from you</u>.　・　　　・よろしくお願いいたします
3. <u>Thank you for your inquiry</u> regarding our products.・　　・～を添付いたします
4. <u>Thank you in advance</u>.　　　　　　　・　　　・お返事をいただければ幸いです

Part 6 Text Completion

次の英文を読み、空所に入れるのに最も適切な語句や文を（A）～（D）から選びましょう。

Questions 5-8 refer to the following e-mail.

To: Philip Martin <pmartin@bioinsight.com>
From: Emily Baker <ebaker@bioinsight.com>
Date: November 10
Subject: Meeting with potential customer

Dear Phil,

I would like to ask you a favor. I ---5.--- with a potential customer, Mr. David Warner, on November 20. I would appreciate it very much if you could be present with me at that meeting, since ---6.--- expertise will be valuable to presenting our products. Mr. Warner is very interested in our technology and eager to meet with us. ---7.--- . I know you will be able to handle them much better than I can. Could you please let me know if November 20 at 3:00 is ---8.--- for you?

Thank you in advance for your help.

Best regards,
Emily

---

5. (A) will be meeting
   (B) have met
   (C) met
   (D) meet

6. (A) our
   (B) his
   (C) my
   (D) your

7. (A) In fact, he asked you some questions.
   (B) However, he decided not to see us.
   (C) He's sure to ask us lots of questions.
   (D) I can handle his questions by myself.

8. (A) convenience
   (B) convenient
   (C) conveniently
   (D) more convenient

オンラインチャットは、基本的に、シングルパッセージ問題の前半に 2 人のやりとりが 1 題、後半に 3 人以上のやりとりが 1 題出題されます。2 人のやりとりは短くて取り組みやすいものが多いですが、3 人以上のやりとりは複雑なので、人物関係やそれぞれの人物が所属する部署を把握するように努めましょう。下の例では、リサとジムのやりとりの途中で加わったマイクは IT チーム所属であることを読み取らなければなりません。

オンラインチャットの例

Lisa Miller [11:08] _____
Jim Beck [11:10] _____
Lisa Miller [11:11] _____
Jim Beck [11:13] _____
Lisa Miller [11:15] Can you tell our IT
　team?
Jim Beck [11:16] Mike, something is
　wrong with our Web site. Can you
　look into it?
Mike McDonald [11:17] No problem.

_____

> IT チームに頼んでほしいというリサの依頼に対して、ジムがマイクに頼んでいることから、マイクはおそらく IT チームであることがわかります。

Part 7 ／ Reading Comprehension

次の英文を読み、設問に対する答えとして最も適切なものを（A）〜（D）から選びましょう。

Questions 9-12 refer to the following online chat discussion.

Aaron Fernandes (10:12 A.M.)

Hi, Dave and Lisa. Have you made arrangements for the conference venue?

David McTominay (10:14 A.M.)

Yes, we have an unconfirmed reservation for room 804. It's a conference room that can accommodate 300 people. It can be used for the main conference on the first day and can be divided into two rooms for 150 people on the second day. Let me know what you think, and I'll make the booking final.

Aaron Fernandes (10:20 A.M.)

Thanks, Dave. I think we're almost ready to finalize the booking. But I recall there was a comment in the preliminary discussions about whether or not we can sell merchandise in the venue. Do we need to pay a higher rate if we engage in commercial activity?

David McTominay (10:23 A.M.)

No, the rate is the same.

Aaron Fernandes (10:24 A.M.)

Great. Also, we'll be expected to pay a deposit. When does the full, final payment need to be made?

David McTominay (10:25 A.M.)

I'm not sure. Lisa, could you confirm the date for me, please?

Lisa Vern (10:27 A.M.)

No problem. I'll do it right away and will get back to you.

---

9. What is the chat discussion mainly about?

(A) A meeting with a new client
(B) A press conference
(C) A reservation
(D) New merchandise

10. According to the chat, what is indicated about the conference?

(A) It will take place over two days.
(B) It was held in room 804.
(C) It turned out to be a great success.
(D) More than 300 people are expected to attend it.

11. The word "venue" in paragraph 1, line 2, is closest in meaning to

(A) date
(B) schedule
(C) payment
(D) place

12. At 10:27 A.M., what does Ms. Vern most likely mean when she writes, "No problem"?

(A) She will make the final payment.
(B) She will check the payment deadline.
(C) She will sell merchandise.
(D) She will confirm the amount of the deposit.

Communicative Training

Part 7 で取り上げたチャットを使ってパートナーと英語で互いに質問をしてみましょう。答える際は、"Yes." や "No." だけで終わらないよう適宜、情報を追加しましょう。

Student A
Student B（パートナー）に下記の質問をしてみましょう。

Student B
Student A（パートナー）の質問に対して Part 7 の英文を見ながら答えましょう。

1. Did Mr. Fernandes make arrangements for the conference venue?
2. How many people can room 804 accommodate?
3. Can the room be divided into two rooms?
4. Do they have to pay a higher rate if they engage in commercial activity?
5. When does the full, final payment need to be made?
6. Who will confirm the date for the final payment?
7. (You choose!)

UNIT 12 Entertainment

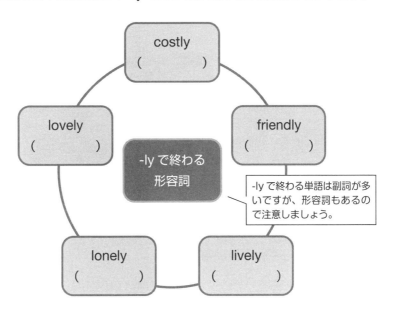 Vocabulary

1. 1 ～ 10 の語句の意味として適切なものを a ～ j の中から選びましょう。　　2-53

1. enforce	_____		a. 緊急事態
2. strictly	_____		b. 厳しく
3. sympathy	_____		c. （小説などの）筋
4. plot	_____		d. つまらない
5. trash	_____		e. 話好きの
6. emergency	_____		f. 実施する
7. dull	_____		g. ～に値する
8. expectation	_____		h. 期待
9. talkative	_____		i. ゴミ
10. deserve	_____		j. 同情

2. 語群の中から適切な日本語訳を選び、-ly で終わる形容詞の図を完成させましょう。

costly
(　　　　　)

lovely
(　　　　　)

friendly
(　　　　　)

-ly で終わる
形容詞

-ly で終わる単語は副詞が多いですが、形容詞もあるので注意しましょう。

lonely
(　　　　　)

lively
(　　　　　)

友好的な　　活発な　　高価な　　孤独な　　愛らしい、素晴らしい

121

Listening Section

Part 1 　解法のコツ　　〈種類を表す名詞〉

写真に写っている物を描写する際に、具体的な名前を挙げずに種類を表す名詞で表現することがあります。例えば、piano の代わりに musical instrument（楽器）を使う場合などです。こうした種類を表す名詞にも慣れておきましょう。

⁞Check⁞

1〜6の単語とその種類を表す語句を線で結びましょう。

1. car	•	• clothing
2. tea	•	• furniture
3. guitar	•	• beverage
4. popcorn	•	• musical instrument
5. chair	•	• vehicle
6. trousers	•	• snack

Part 1 　**Photographs**　　　　　　　　　　 2-54, 55

（A）〜（D）の英文を聞き、写真を最も適切に描写しているものを選びましょう。

1.

(A)　　　(B)　　　(C)　　　(D)

Part 2 　解法のコツ　　〈あいまいな応答〉

問いかけに対して、「どちらでも構わない」、「別の人に聞いてほしい」、「もう少し考えさせてほしい」のように、あいまいな応答が正解となることもあります。

　　問いかけ　　　　Should we start production next week or next month?
　　正解の応答例　　Talk to the manager.

Part 2 **Question-Response**

最初に聞こえてくる英文に対する応答として最も適切なものを（A）〜（C）から選びましょう。

2. Mark your answer.　　(A)　　　(B)　　　(C)
3. Mark your answer.　　(A)　　　(B)　　　(C)
4. Mark your answer.　　(A)　　　(B)　　　(C)

Part 3 解法のコツ 〈**3人での会話**〉

会話は基本的に2人ですが、全部で13ある会話のうち2つ程度は3人の会話となっています。その場合、"Questions XX through XX refer to the following conversation with three speakers." という指示文が会話の前に流れ、3人の会話であることがわかるようになっています。2人の会話と3人の会話で解き方に大きな違いはありませんが、1人しかいない性別に関する設問が多いので、その人の発言に注意しましょう。また、設問に具体的な人名が出てくることも特徴の1つです。

ex.）男性1名、女性2名の会話における設問例

・Who is the man?
　　　　　⇒1名しか登場しない性別に関する設問が目立つ！

・What does Janet Potter inquire about?
　　　　　⇒同じ性別が複数いるため、人名が記載されることが多い！

Part 3 **Conversations**

 2-60〜62

会話を聞き、5〜7の設問に対する解答として最も適切なものを（A）〜（D）から選びましょう。

5. What is true about Marcos Pepin?

(A) He left his band to be a solo singer.
(B) He had a heart attack.
(C) He has some throat trouble.
(D) He has lost his hearing.

6. What does the woman mean when she says, "But our tickets"?

(A) She is worried that the tickets will become worthless.
(B) She is concerned that she has left the tickets at home.
(C) She has found the tickets.
(D) She has lost the tickets.

7. What does Bill say he is not sure about?

(A) What he said about Marcos Pepin
(B) What John said about the gig
(C) Whether Marcos Pepin can sing next month or not
(D) Whether he can go to the rearranged gig or not

Part 4 　**解法のコツ**　〈オリエンテーション／ツアー〉

オリエンテーションやツアーの案内では、下記のような基本的な流れがあります。予定が順番に話されるので、時刻や場所を聞き漏らさないに注意しましょう。

1. 呼びかけ　Hello, my name is Luke and I'll be your museum guide this afternoon.
⇒ツアーの場所は美術館！

2. 予定　We'll start by visiting a special exhibition of impressionist painters for an hour until about 2 P.M.
⇒最初は特別展を鑑賞予定！

3. 注意事項　Please remember, you're not allowed to take photos of the art works.
⇒写真撮影は禁止！

4. 結び　OK, let's begin. Please follow me.
⇒ツアーの開始！

Part 4 　**Talks**　 2-63〜65

トークを聞き、8 〜 10 の設問に対する解答として最も適切なものを（A）〜（D）から選びましょう。

8. Where would you hear this talk?

(A) At a sports game
(B) At a movie theater
(C) At a museum
(D) At a music festival

9. What is the first rule the speaker mentioned?

(A) Throw your trash in the recycling bins.
(B) Wear your wristbands at all times.
(C) Check the emergency exits.
(D) Wait at the back of the venue.

10. What will most likely happen after this talk?

(A) People will pick up trash off the street.
(B) People will buy wristbands.
(C) A festival will begin.
(D) A soccer game will start.

Communicative Training

1. Part 2のスクリプトにある最初の問いかけを使ってパートナーと英語で互いに質問をしてみましょう。質問に答える際は、下の回答例を参考にしましょう。なお、スクリプトは教員から配布されます。

Student A
Student B（パートナー）に Part 2 のスクリプトにある最初の問いかけをしてみましょう。

Student B
Student A（パートナー）の質問に対して下の回答例を参考に答えましょう。

Q2
・はい、学生証*を見せてください。*student ID card
・いいえ、ございません。
・すみませんが、他の人に聞いてください。
・(You choose!)

Q3
・いいえ、どうぞ。
・ええ、私の友人がすぐに戻ってきます。
・よくわかりません。
・(You choose!)

Q4
・すみません。
・そうでしたか？ 知りませんでした。
・あの男の人は（写真を撮っても）良いと言いましたよ。
・(You choose!)

2. Part 3の対話スクリプトの内容について、パートナーと英語で互いに質問をしてみましょう。質問に答える際は、対話スクリプトだけを見るようにし、下の質問は見ないようにしましょう。なお、スクリプトは教員から配布されます。

Student A
Student B（パートナー）に下記の質問をしてみましょう。

Student B
Student A（パートナー）の質問に対して Part 3 の対話スクリプトを見ながら答えましょう。

1. Why was the concert canceled?
2. What does the woman say about their tickets?
3. When will the rearranged gig be held?
4. Does she want to get a refund, or go to the rearranged gig?
5. (You choose!)

 **Reading Section**

> Help (you / your / yours / yourself) to anything on the table.

この問題は、選択肢を見ると代名詞問題と言えますが、help oneself to（〜を自由に取って食べる）という慣用句の知識があればすぐに解けます。語彙学習の際は単語だけでなく、こうした慣用句にも注意を払いましょう。

⋛Check⋛

1〜4の英文中で下線を引いた語句とその日本語訳とを線で結びましょう。

1. Come in and <u>make yourself at home</u>.　•　•笑いものになる
2. I don't want to <u>make a fool of myself</u>.　•　•思わず
3. Jack <u>prides himself on</u> his singing.　•　•くつろぐ
4. Janet laughed <u>in spite of herself</u>.　•　•〜を自慢する

Part 5　Incomplete Sentences

英文を完成させるのに最も適切な語句を（A）〜（D）から選びましょう。

1. I just can't help ------- out loud every time I see his films.

  (A) laugh
  (B) laughing
  (C) to laugh
  (D) laughed

2. Mr. Murray devoted ------- to his entertainment business.

  (A) he
  (B) his
  (C) him
  (D) himself

3. As far as commercial success is ------- , his latest movie failed to meet our expectations.

  (A) concerned
  (B) worried
  (C) permitted
  (D) connected

4. When it ------- to movies, nobody can beat Fred.

  (A) come
  (B) came
  (C) comes
  (D) coming

語句挿入問題では、Part 5 同様に前置詞問題がありますが、as for（〜に関しては）のような群前置詞が選択肢に並ぶことも多くあります。群前置詞とは、2 語以上の単語がつながって、1 つの前置詞のように使われる表現ですが、because of（〜のために）など、頻出のものは確実にチェックしておきましょう。

⚞Check⚟

1〜4 の英文中で下線を引いた語句とその日本語訳とを線で結びましょう。

1. We employ people <u>regardless of</u> race, age, sex or gender. •　　• 〜の場合には
2. Raymond speaks French <u>in addition to</u> Spanish. •　　• 〜にかかわらず
3. Dial 911 <u>in case of</u> emergency. •　　• 〜に加えて
4. The bus was delayed <u>due to</u> heavy snow. •　　• 〜のために

Part 6　Text Completion

次の英文を読み、空所に入れるのに最も適切な語句や文を（A）〜（D）から選びましょう。

Questions 5-8 refer to the following advertisement.

Enjoy a movie in the park!

Hollywood stars return to Denver this summer, as Movies in the Parks
brings big-screen entertainment to local parks for the tenth season.
Public health guidelines, ------- the wearing of face masks, will be strictly enforced
5.
to ensure the health and safety of all who attend. ------- .
6.
Check our Web site to ------- which movies are playing.
7.
All movies begin ------- 8:00 P.M.
8.

---

5. (A) including
(B) despite
(C) through
(D) instead of

6. (A) You can enjoy Hollywood movies at home.
(B) Please review the health guidelines every moviegoer must follow.
(C) Our Web site is temporarily closed for maintenance.
(D) Call (312) 123-4567 for weather-related cancellations.

7. (A) choose
(B) reserve
(C) find out
(D) pay

8. (A) through
(B) in
(C) on
(D) at

Part 7 は限られた時間で大量の英文を読む必要があるので時間との戦いになります。その中でも特に時間がかかるのが、「〜でないものはどれですか？」というタイプの設問です。選択肢 (A) 〜 (D) のそれぞれについて文書の中に記載があるかどうかを確認していかなければならないので、どうしても解答に時間がかかります。実際の試験の場合にはこうした設問は後回しにするなどして時間を有効に活用しましょう。

設問例

・What is NOT true about A?

・What is NOT mentioned as a feature of A?

・What does NOT apply to A?

> 時間がない時は「〜でないもの」タイプの設問は後回しにするのも1つの手段です！

Part 7 　Reading Comprehension

次の英文を読み、設問に対する答えとして最も適切なものを（A）〜（D）から選びましょう。

Questions 9-12 refer to the following article.

Planes, Trains, Automobiles, and Ships

Rating 　Highly recommended 　★★★★★★★★★☆ (9/10)

Plot

Dave (Martin Scott) is a stressed-out businessman, trying to get home to spend Thanksgiving with his family. He's having trouble getting a taxi to the airport, but does he have problems? Not really, not until he meets friendly and talkative shower curtain ring salesman Pete Hughes (John Griffiths). That's when Dave's problems really begin! As heavy snow forces the cancellation of their flight, this odd couple end up having to find their way home together.

Review

Planes, Trains, Automobiles, and Ships is a hilarious comedy, with outstanding performances by Scott and Griffiths. It's a road movie with some unexpected plot twists and a superb soundtrack. Dave and Pete's adventure is always believable and never dull. These immensely likeable characters deserve our sympathy and 90 minutes of our time.

9. What most likely is *Planes, Trains, Automobiles, and Ships*?

    (A) A play
    (B) A film
    (C) An online game
    (D) A book

10. What is mentioned about Dave?

    (A) He sells shower curtain rings.
    (B) His character is played by John Griffiths.
    (C) He is trying to get home with his family.
    (D) He has to travel with Mr. Hughes.

11. The word "outstanding" in paragraph 2, line 1, is closest in meaning to

    (A) ordinary
    (B) poor
    (C) excellent
    (D) serious

12. What is NOT indicated about *Planes, Trains, Automobiles, and Ships*?

    (A) It lasts more than two hours.
    (B) It is a road movie.
    (C) It stars Martin Scott and John Griffiths.
    (D) It is a very good comedy.

Communicative Training

Part 7 で取り上げた記事を使ってパートナーと英語で互いに質問をしてみましょう。答える際は、"Yes." や "No." だけで終わらないよう適宜、情報を追加しましょう。

Student A
Student B（パートナー）に下記の質問をしてみましょう。

Student B
Student A（パートナー）の質問に対して Part 7 の英文を見ながら答えましょう。

1. Who is starring in *Planes, Trains, Automobiles, and Ships*?
2. Who is Pete Hughes?
3. Who plays the character of Pete Hughes?
4. What kind of movie is *Planes, Trains, Automobiles, and Ships*?
5. How long is the movie?
6. How is the rating for the movie?
7. (You choose!)

本テキストで取り上げている定型表現一覧

　イベントの発表、告知などを扱った英文では、「〜をお知らせいたします」や「〜で開催されます」のような定型表現が数多く出てきます。こうした定型表現に慣れておくと、Part 6 や Part 7 といったリーディングセクションだけでなく、Part 4 のようなリスニングセクションでも役立ちます。次の表を使って本テキストで取り上げている定型表現を確認しましょう。

	例文	下線部の意味
イベントの発表、告知	Macy's is pleased to announce the opening of its new store.	〜を発表いたします
	Visitors are encouraged to use public transportation.	〜をご利用ください
	The concert takes place next Thursday.	開催される
	His latest movie features an all-star cast.	〜を呼びものとする
求人案内	Please send your résumé to Kate Ross.	履歴書を送る
	Applicants must have a university degree in tourism.	応募者には〜が必要です
	Duties include frequent visits to clients.	職務には〜が含まれます
	We are looking for someone with a background in marketing.	〜の経歴がある
eメールや手紙	Please find attached the schedule for the seminar.	〜を添付いたします
	I look forward to hearing from you.	お返事をいただければ幸いです
	Thank you for your inquiry regarding our products.	お問い合わせありがとうございます
	Thank you in advance.	よろしくお願いいたします
保守点検等の告知	Please be informed that we will be closed on December 25 for Christmas.	〜をお知らせします
	Thank you for your patience and cooperation.	ご辛抱
	The programs may change without notice.	予告なしに
	We apologize for any inconvenience this may cause you.	ご迷惑

We apologize for any inconvenience this may cause you.

UNIT 13 Education

 Vocabulary

1. 1 ～ 10 の語句の意味として適切なものを a ～ j の中から選びましょう。　　🔊 2-66

1. committee	＿＿＿＿	a. 目的
2. assignment	＿＿＿＿	b. 特別に、とりわけ
3. intend	＿＿＿＿	c. 集中的な
4. academic	＿＿＿＿	d. 委員会
5. maintain	＿＿＿＿	e. 学業成績の
6. senior	＿＿＿＿	f. ～を探索する
7. objective	＿＿＿＿	g. ～を意図する
8. intensive	＿＿＿＿	h. 宿題、課題
9. particularly	＿＿＿＿	i. 維持する
10. explore	＿＿＿＿	j. （大学の）4 年生

2. 語群の中から下線部の単語の品詞と適切な日本語訳を選び、表を完成させましょう。

単語	例文	品詞	日本語訳
late	It's too <u>late</u> to start complaining now.		
	The bus came ten minutes <u>late</u>.		
lately	I haven't been feeling so well <u>lately</u>.		
hard	She's a very <u>hard</u> worker.		
	I kicked the ball as <u>hard</u> as I could.		
hardly	We <u>hardly</u> know each other.		

【品詞】
形容詞　　副詞

【日本語訳】
強く　　最近　　ほとんど～ない　　一生懸命な　　遅れて　　遅い

・-ly は副詞を作る接尾辞ですが、hardly や lately は意味に注意しましょう。
・late や hard は形容詞と副詞のどちらにも使われます。early や fast なども同様です。

Part 1 　解法のコツ　〈すべての選択肢の確認〉

写真の中で目立つものはキーワードになりやすいですが、多くの場合、複数の選択肢で使われます。最初に聞こえてきたものに飛びつかず、すべての選択肢を確認したうえで解答しましょう。

⁘Check⁘

下の写真の描写として最も適切な英文を1～4の中から選びましょう。

1. The man is <u>putting on</u> a hat.
2. The man is <u>looking for</u> a hat.
3. The man is waving his hand.
4. The man is <u>wearing</u> a hat.

> キーワードは hat ですが、3つの文に使われており、正答の決め手になるのは下線部です。

Part 1 　Photographs 　　　　　　　　　　　CD 2-67, 68

(A)～(D) の英文を聞き、写真を最も適切に描写しているものを選びましょう。

1.

(A)　　(B)　　(C)　　(D)

Part 2 　解法のコツ　〈主語が異なる応答〉

Wh 疑問文や Yes/No 疑問文が中心になるので、出だしに着目することが重要ですが、主語が何かも確認しておきましょう。"Yes, I did." が正解となるべき質問に対して、"Yes, he did." のように、主語が間違っている選択肢が用意されていることがあります。

問いかけ	What did they discuss at the meeting?
不正解の応答例	We talked about the new product.
正解の応答例	They talked about the budget.

最初に聞こえてくる英文に対する応答として最も適切なものを（A）〜（C）から選びましょう。

2. Mark your answer.   (A)   (B)   (C)

3. Mark your answer.   (A)   (B)   (C)

4. Mark your answer.   (A)   (B)   (C)

Part 3 / 解法のコツ 〈図表問題**2**〉

図表問題は、会話から得られる情報と図表から得られる情報を組み合わせないと解けない仕組みになっています。図表問題の場合、図表にざっと目を通し、どんな情報が載っているのかを会話が流れてくる前に確認しておきましょう。

図表の情報：部屋番号と科目名

Room	Subject
101	
102	French Literature
201	
202	Intercultural Communication
203	
301	
302	Philosophy

7. Look at the graphic. Where will Professor Jackson's class most likely be held?

(A) Room 101
(B) Room 201
(C) Room 203
(D) Room 301

選択肢が部屋番号なので、会話に出てくる科目名を聞き逃さないようにしましょう！

Part 3 / **Conversations** 2-73〜75

会話を聞き、5〜7の設問に対する解答として最も適切なものを（A）〜（D）から選びましょう。

Room	Subject
101	
102	French Literature
201	
202	Intercultural Communication
203	
301	
302	Philosophy

5. What does the man want to do?

(A) Cancel his class
(B) Borrow a projector
(C) Change the classroom
(D) Help the woman

6. According to the man, what is the problem?

(A) The room is too small.
(B) The screen is too small.
(C) The air conditioner isn't working.
(D) Students haven't registered for the course.

7. Look at the graphic. Where will Professor Jackson's class most likely be held?

(A) Room 101
(B) Room 201
(C) Room 203
(D) Room 301

表彰式や講演会などでこれから登場する人を紹介するスピーチには、下記のような基本的な流れがあるので、情報がどのような順序で出てくるか予測することができます。慣れておきましょう。

1. 呼びかけ　Good evening and welcome to Radio KRV's Thursday night lecture series.
　　⇒番組名の連絡

2. 目的　Tonight, we are fortunate to have with us Dr. Emma Fielding.
　　⇒ゲストの紹介

3. 追加情報　She is the author of three books on early childhood education.
　　⇒肩書、経歴、テーマなど、ゲストに関する追加情報の紹介

4. 結び　Welcome to the show, Dr. Fielding.
　　⇒ゲストへのバトンタッチ

Part 4 **Talks**

 2-76〜78

トークを聞き、8 〜 10 の設問に対する解答として最も適切なものを（A）〜（D）から選びましょう。

8. What is the purpose of the talk?

(A) To advertise a book
(B) To tell a story about UNICEF
(C) To introduce a speaker
(D) To introduce himself

9. What will Dave Jennings most likely talk about?

(A) Teaching
(B) His work with UNICEF
(C) His research
(D) Business

10. How long has Dave Jennings served as an adviser?

(A) Over 20 years
(B) About 15 years
(C) About 10 years
(D) About 5 years

Communicative Training

1. Part 2 のスクリプトにある最初の問いかけを使ってパートナーと英語で互いに質問をしてみましょう。質問に答える際は、下の回答例を参考にしましょう。なお、スクリプトは教員から配布されます。

Student A
Student B（パートナー）に Part 2 のスクリプトにある最初の問いかけをしてみましょう。

Student B
Student A（パートナー）の質問に対して下の回答例を参考に答えましょう。

Q2	Q3	Q4
・彼女はとてもよくやっていますよ。 ・彼女はよく遅刻しますね。 ・彼女はクラスで1番優秀な生徒です。 ・(You choose!)	・(それは) 次の金曜日が締め切りです。 ・まだ決めていません。 ・(それは) 昨日が締め切りでした。 ・(You choose!)	・はい、もちろんです。 ・はい、後で私のオフィスに来てください。 ・すみません、できません。 ・(You choose!)

2. Part 3 の対話スクリプトの内容について、パートナーと英語で互いに質問をしてみましょう。質問に答える際は、対話スクリプトだけを見るようにし、下の質問は見ないようにしましょう。なお、スクリプトは教員から配布されます。

Student A
Student B（パートナー）に下記の質問をしてみましょう。

Student B
Student A（パートナー）の質問に対して Part 3 の対話スクリプトを見ながら答えましょう。

1. Who is teaching Intercultural Communication?
2. How many students does he have in his class?
3. Does he want to use room 202? Why or why not?
4. What does the woman say about the new room?
5. (You choose!)

 **Reading Section**

代名詞問題には、人称代名詞の他に関係代名詞も含まれます。関係代名詞の問題の場合は、まず空所の前を見て、先行詞にあたる名詞（句）が人であるか、それとも人以外であるかを確認します。次に、空所の後の部分がどのような構造になっているかを見極めましょう。
また、下の図を参考にして主な関係代名詞について確認しておきましょう。

先行詞	主格	所有格	目的格
人	who	whose	who / whom
人以外	which	whose	which
人・人以外	that	−	that

> 目的格の関係代名詞は省略されることもあります。

✎Check✎

下線部に注意して、1〜4の英文中のカッコ内から正しい語を選び○で囲みましょう。

1. Can you see the house (who / whose / which) <u>roof is red</u>?
2. Is there anyone (who / whose / which) <u>can answer this question</u>?
3. Ms. Parker teaches them everything (who / whose / that) <u>they want to know</u>.
4. We have math homework (who / whose / that) <u>is due tomorrow</u>.

Part 5　Incomplete Sentences

英文を完成させるのに最も適切な語句を（A）〜（D）から選びましょう。

1. This course is intended for students ------- are interested in health-related careers.
- (A) those
- (B) they
- (C) which
- (D) who

2. The carpet in the school library will be replaced with material ------- is easier to maintain.
- (A) this
- (B) that
- (C) whose
- (D) what

3. Jane's parents, ------- are both professors, work at the same college.
- (A) who
- (B) which
- (C) that
- (D) what

4. Students ------- academic performance is unsatisfactory will receive a letter from the school this month.
- (A) who
- (B) whom
- (C) whose
- (D) that

Unit 12 で取り上げた群前置詞同様に、群接続詞が選択肢に並ぶことも多くあります。群接続詞とは、2 語以上の単語がつながって、1 つの接続詞のように使われる表現ですが、as soon as（〜したらすぐに）など、頻出のものは確実にチェックしておきましょう。

Check

1 〜 4 の英文中で下線を引いた語句とその日本語訳とを線で結びましょう。

1. <u>Now that</u> the kids have left home, we have a lot of
   extra space.   •   • 〜の限りは
2. You can stay here, <u>as long as</u> you keep quiet.   •   • たとえ〜であっても
3. <u>Even if</u> you take a taxi, you'll still miss your train. •   • 〜する時までに
4. <u>By the time</u> I got to the party, people had already left. •   • 今や〜なので

Part 6 Text Completion

次の英文を読み、空所に入れるのに最も適切な語句や文を（A）〜（D）から選びましょう。

Questions 5-8 refer to the following notice.

The Career Center is the perfect place to start your career search. -------- you're
5.
a first-year student or a senior getting ready for that next step, our staff will
work -------- with you in order to meet your career objectives. We will provide the
6.
support and resources -------- to make your career exploration and employment
7.
search successful. -------- .
8.

5. (A) Even though
(B) Unless
(C) Whether
(D) As long as

6. (A) directly
(B) direct
(C) direction
(D) director

7. (A) need
(B) needed
(C) needing
(D) have needed

8. (A) This used to be a great opportunity to meet
employers.
(B) Congratulations on getting a job before
graduation.
(C) This workshop features top business
professionals.
(D) To arrange a time to discuss your specific
needs, please call 123-456-7890.

137

ダブルパッセージ問題では、両方の文書を読まないと解けない形式の問題（クロスレファレンス問題）が必ず含まれます。次の例では、文書Aで会議の開始時間を読み取り、文書Bでスミス氏が30分遅れることを読み取って初めて正解の（D）にたどり着けます。慣れるまでは難しいですが、問題を数多くこなしながらコツを掴みましょう。

What time will Mr. Smith attend the meeting?
- (A) 2:00
- (B) 2:30
- (C) 3:00
- (D) 3:30

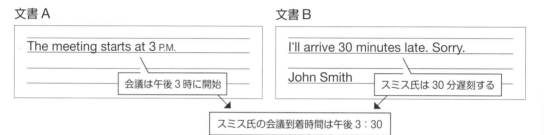

文書A

The meeting starts at 3 P.M.

会議は午後3時に開始

文書B

I'll arrive 30 minutes late. Sorry.

John Smith

スミス氏は30分遅刻する

スミス氏の会議到着時間は午後3：30

Part 7 Reading Comprehension

次の英文を読み、設問に対する答えとして最も適切なものを（A）～（D）から選びましょう。

Questions 9-13 refer to the following Web page and e-mail.

WESTCHESTER COMMUNITY COLLEGE

Home	Adult Education Courses	Registration / Term Dates	Access / Contact us

Life skills, career development, and a clear vision for your future!
Returning to learning as a mature student can have many benefits, both for your life and your career.

Come and join our Adult Courses and benefit from quality education in a supportive environment. Courses starting next month include … (click here for full list)

Introduction to Counseling
This 4-week course aims to improve your communication skills and to provide a basic understanding of what counseling is.

Applied Science and Technology
This 2-week intensive program offers the chance to enhance your employment opportunities through digital skills training.

Computers for Beginners
In this 4-week course, you will learn how to use a mouse and a keyboard, and how to use basic software. This class is for those with little or no computer experience.

Social Media for Career Changers

This 2-week intensive program helps you to learn how to use social media to search for employment.

To:	contact@westchestercc.com
From:	d.cooper@maccjobs.com
Date:	December 18th
Subject:	Adult Education Courses

Dear Sir or Madam,

I am recently retired and am interested in exploring new areas that would enable me to extend my working life. I am particularly interested in your 4-week courses. However, I have recently celebrated my 60th birthday. Could you kindly advise me whether you have any upper-age limits for your courses? I should also add that my IT skills are not particularly good, and I am not interested in developing these skills. Would this be a particular handicap for these courses?

Kind regards,

Damian Cooper

9. On the Web page, what is indicated about courses offered by Westchester Community College?

(A) Advertised courses start next month.
(B) They are all intended for retired people.
(C) They are all related to computer skills.
(D) They are all 4-week courses.

10. On the Web page, the word "mature" in paragraph 1, line 2, is closest in meaning to

(A) part-time
(B) full-time
(C) scholarship
(D) adult

11. What is the purpose of the e-mail?

(A) To register for a course
(B) To apply for a job opening
(C) To make inquiries
(D) To recommend a course

12. According to the e-mail, what is true about Mr. Cooper?

(A) He is interested in learning IT skills.
(B) He used to teach at Westchester Community College.
(C) He will turn 60 before long.
(D) He is unemployed now.

13. What course would Mr. Cooper most likely be interested in taking?

(A) Computers for Beginners
(B) Introduction to Counseling
(C) Applied Science and Technology
(D) Social Media for Career Changers

Part 7 で取り上げたウェブページと e メールを使ってパートナーと英語で互いに質問をして
みましょう。答える際は、"Yes." や "No." だけで終わらないよう適宜、情報を追加しましょう。

Student A
Student B（パート
ナー）に下記の質問
をしてみましょう。

Student B
Student A（パート
ナー）の質問に対し
て Part 7 の英文を見
ながら答えましょう。

1. Does Westchester Community College offer adult
   education courses?
2. How long is Introduction to Counseling?
3. What is the purpose of Introduction to Counseling?
4. What courses are two-week intensive programs?
5. How old is Mr. Cooper?
6. What does he write about his IT skills?
7. (You choose!)

UNIT 14 Housing

 Vocabulary

1. 1 ～ 10 の語句の意味として適切なものを a ～ j の中から選びましょう。　🎵 2-79

1. resident	_____	a.	保険
2. inspection	_____	b.	契約（書）
3. landlord	_____	c.	検査
4. real estate	_____	d.	宿泊施設
5. accommodation	_____	e.	～を明確にする
6. insurance	_____	f.	居住者
7. contract	_____	g.	不動産
8. clarify	_____	h.	家賃
9. rent	_____	i.	団地
10. development	_____	j.	家主、大家

2. 語群の中から下線部の単語の品詞と適切な日本語訳を選び、表を完成させましょう。

単語	例文	品詞	日本語訳
interest	This may be of particular <u>interest</u> to you.		
	I have some news that might <u>interest</u> you.		
	How much <u>interest</u> are you paying on the loan?		
rise	House prices began to <u>rise</u> rapidly last year.		
	We are expecting a <u>rise</u> in interest rates.		
fine	If it's <u>fine</u> tomorrow, we'll go out.		
	Jim had to pay a $200 <u>fine</u> for speeding.		

【品詞】

名詞　動詞　形容詞

【日本語訳】

晴れた　上昇する　金利　罰金　興味　上昇　～に興味を持たせる

単語の中には複数の品詞を取るものが多くあるので注意しましょう！

Listening Section

Part 1 　解法のコツ　〈物の状態〉

〈物〉が中心の写真の場合には、その「位置」と「状態」を確認しましょう。位置関係は、前置詞がポイントになりますが、状態について「積み重ねられている」、「立て掛けられている」などの頻出表現をチェックしておきましょう。

Books are piled up / stacked. （本が積み重ねられています）	A skateboard is leaning against the wall. （スケートボードが壁に立て掛けられています）	A clock is hanging on the wall. （時計が壁に掛かっています）

Part 1 　Photographs　　　　　🎧 2-80, 81

(A) 〜 (D) の英文を聞き、写真を最も適切に描写しているものを選びましょう。

1.

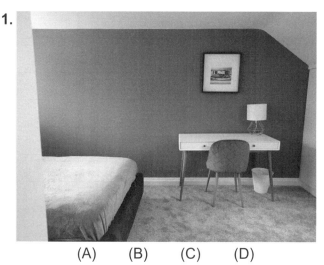

(A)　　(B)　　(C)　　(D)

Part 2 　解法のコツ　〈質問で返す応答〉

問いかけに対して、「誰から聞いたのですか？」のように、質問で返す応答が正解となる場合があります。自然なやりとりになるように、最初の問いかけから対話の場面を想像することが大切です。

　　問いかけ　　　Should we have Chinese food or Italian food?
　　正解の応答例　What's less expensive?

最初に聞こえてくる英文に対する応答として最も適切なものを（A）～（C）から選びましょう。

2. Mark your answer.　　(A)　　(B)　　(C)
3. Mark your answer.　　(A)　　(B)　　(C)
4. Mark your answer.　　(A)　　(B)　　(C)

Part 3 / 解法のコツ　　〈意図を問う設問〉

設問の中には、会話で使われた表現を引用し、「～と言った時、男性は何を意味していますか？」のように、話者の意図を尋ねるものがあります。文字どおりの意味ではなく、会話の文脈の中でその表現がどのように使われているかをよく考えましょう。また、こうした設問には次のようないくつかのパターンがあります。

・What does the man mean when he says "I think it ticks all your boxes"?
　　⇒「何を意味しているのか？」
・What does the man imply when he says "I think it ticks all your boxes"?
　　⇒「何をほのめかしているのか？」
・Why does the man say, "I think it ticks all your boxes"?
　　⇒「なぜ～と言うのか？」

Part 3 / **Conversations** 2-86～88

会話を聞き、5 ～ 7 の設問に対する解答として最も適切なものを（A）～（D）から選びましょう。

Floor Plan

		1008		
1001	1002		1004	

5. What most likely is the man's job?

(A) Furniture retailer
(B) Architect
(C) Travel agent
(D) Real estate agent

6. What does the man mean when he says "I think it ticks all your boxes"?

(A) It is the largest apartment.
(B) It has a great view.
(C) It has everything the woman wants.
(D) It is recommended by a lot of people.

7. Look at the graphic. Which apartment are the speakers talking about?

(A) 1001
(B) 1002
(C) 1004
(D) 1008

商品やサービスの広告に関するトークの場合、相手の注意を引くために最初の呼びかけで概要がわかるようになっています。下記が基本的な流れなので、特に出だしに注意して聞くようにしましょう。

	1. 呼びかけ	Are you looking to buy or rent a home in the Pinnacle City area? ⇒対象は家の購入や賃貸を検討している人
	2. 自己紹介	The real estate agents here at Apex Real Estate can help. ⇒社名の紹介
	3. 詳細	We'll find an apartment or house that suits you. ⇒業務の紹介
	4. 追加情報	We'll give you a free gift card that you can use for purchases at the Pinnacle Home Improvement Store. ⇒特典としてギフトを進呈
	5. 結び	Just stop by our office today! ⇒聞き手への提案

Part 4　Talks

 2-89〜91

トークを聞き、8 〜 10 の設問に対する解答として最も適切なものを（A）〜（D）から選びましょう。

8. Who is this advertisement directed to?

(A) People who want to rent a house
(B) People who have trouble paying back a loan
(C) People who need to lease a house
(D) People who are interested in buying a house

9. What is Kingsfield Estate?

(A) A housing development
(B) A real-estate company
(C) A private house
(D) An apartment building

10. What are the listeners asked to do on July 12th?

(A) Hold an open house
(B) Join an event
(C) Call Dream Homes
(D) Fill out a form

1. Part 2 のスクリプトにある最初の問いかけを使ってパートナーと英語で互いに質問をしてみましょう。質問に答える際は、下の回答例を参考にしましょう。なお、スクリプトは教員から配布されます。

Student A
Student B（パートナー）に Part 2 のスクリプトにある最初の問いかけをしてみましょう。

Student B
Student A（パートナー）の質問に対して下の回答例を参考に答えましょう。

Q2
・月 400 ドルです。
・昨年と同じです。
・まだ決めていません。
・（You choose!）

Q3
・はい、先週引っ越しました。
・誰から聞いたのですか？
（＝誰があなたに話したのですか？）
・いいえ、引っ越していません。
・（You choose!）

Q4
・はい、たくさんあります。
・はい、通りの先に*1 つあります。　*down the street
・すみません、この辺のことはよく知りません。
・（You choose!）

2. Part 3 の対話スクリプトの内容について、パートナーと英語で互いに質問をしてみましょう。質問に答える際は、対話スクリプトだけを見るようにし、下の質問は見ないようにしましょう。なお、スクリプトは教員から配布されます。

Student A
Student B（パートナー）に下記の質問をしてみましょう。

Student B
Student A（パートナー）の質問に対して Part 3 の対話スクリプトを見ながら答えましょう。

1. Does the woman think the apartment is too small?
2. Is the apartment far from the station?
3. On what floor is the apartment?
4. What does the man say about the view from the apartment?
5. (You choose!)

Reading Section

Part 5　解法のコツ　〈動詞の形問題 **4**〉

「彼が来たら知らせてください」における「彼が来たら」の部分は未来のことを指していますが、"Call me when he comes." のように現在形を使います。このように、時を表す when や条件を表す if などで始まる副詞節では、未来のことであっても will ではなく現在時制を使うので注意しましょう。ただし、名詞節の場合には、未来のことを表す場合には will を使うので気をつけてください。

> 2つ以上の単語のまとまりが１つの品詞と同じ働きをするもののうち、主語と動詞を含むものを節と呼び、主語と動詞を含まないものは句と呼びます。

副詞節	副詞の役割を果たす節で、修飾語になります。 ex.) Call me **when he comes**.
名詞節	名詞の役割を果たす節で、主語や目的語になります。 ex.) I don't know **when he will come**.

☆Check☆

1 ～ 3 の英文中のカッコ内から正しい語句を選び○で囲みましょう。

1. If you (have / will have) time tomorrow, let's have dinner at my house.

2. Ted won't go to sleep unless you (tell / will tell) him a story.

3. Does anyone know when the taxi (is / will be) here?

Part 5 Incomplete Sentences

英文を完成させるのに最も適切な語句を（A）～（D）から選びましょう。

1. I will call you when I ------- up my mind to rent the apartment.

(A) make
(B) will make
(C) made
(D) making

2. Our landlord ------- our rent when we said we might move out.

(A) has lowered
(B) lowers
(C) will lower
(D) lowered

3. As soon as the ad appeared in the paper, we ------- many inquiries about the office for rent.

(A) receive
(B) received
(C) will receive
(D) receiving

4. Steve is staying in temporary accommodation until his house ------- rebuilt.

(A) will be
(B) was
(C) is
(D) is being

Part 6 解法のコツ 〈定型表現 4〉

保守点検の告知などを扱った英文では、「ご不便をおかけし、申し訳ございません」や「ご協力のほど、よろしくお願い申し上げます」のような定型表現が数多く登場します。こうした定型表現が語句挿入の問題に使われることもあるので、ぜひ慣れておきましょう。

☆Check☆

1 ～ 4 の英文中で下線を引いた語句とその日本語訳とを線で結びましょう。

1. Please be informed that we will be closed on December 25 for Christmas.   •   • 予告なしに

2. Thank you for your patience and cooperation.   •   • ～をお知らせします

3. The programs may change without notice.   •   • ご迷惑

4. We apologize for any inconvenience this may cause.   •   • ご辛抱

147

Part 6 **Text Completion**

次の英文を読み、空所に入れるのに最も適切な語句や文を（A）～（D）から選びましょう。

Questions 5-8 refer to the following notice.

Power Outage Notice

All residents,

Please be informed that on Tuesday, November 7 there will be a scheduled power outage ---5.--- annual facility/equipment inspection work. The work ---6.--- to begin at 1 P.M. and be finished ---7.--- 5 P.M. the same day.

We apologize for any inconvenience this may cause. ---8.--- .

---

5. (A) thanks to
　　 (B) regardless of
　　 (C) due to
　　 (D) with respect to

6. (A) expects
　　 (B) expected
　　 (C) expecting
　　 (D) is expected

7. (A) by
　　 (B) on
　　 (C) until
　　 (D) from

8. (A) We are looking forward to meeting you then.
　　 (B) Thank you for your understanding and cooperation.
　　 (C) This power outage will last for a week.
　　 (D) We are pleased to inform you of this problem.

トリプルパッセージ問題では、クロスレファレンス問題が5問中2〜3問含まれます。1つの問題を解くのに3つの文書A〜Cのすべてから情報を組み合わせないといけないことはまれです。文書Aと文書C、文書Bと文書Cのように、2つの文書に含まれる情報を組み合わせて解く形式になっており、基本的にはダブルパッセージ問題と変わりません。ただし、やはり難しいですので、少しずつ慣れていきましょう。

文書A（会議の開催通知）

The meeting starts at 3 P.M.

文書B（道路閉鎖の通知）

ROAD CLOSED

文書C（スミス氏のeメール）

I'll arrive 30 minutes late. Sorry.

John Smith

10. What time will Mr. Smith attend the meeting? — 文書Aと文書Cの情報が必要！
    (A) 2:00
    (B) 2:30
    (C) 3:00
    (D) 3:30

11. Why will Mr. Smith be late for the meeting? — 文書Bと文書Cの情報が必要！
    (A) He has to go see a doctor.
    (B) He has to attend another meeting.
    (C) His car broke down.
    (D) He has to take another route.

次の英文を読み、設問に対する答えとして最も適切なものを（A）〜（D）から選びましょう。

Questions 9-13 refer to the following Web page and two e-mails.

Everglade Drive, Peytonville
4-bedroomed home to rent

In Everglade Drive you'll find the charming, pet-friendly residence you've been looking for. Live in a four-bedroom, two-bathroom home with attached garage. Surrounded by green space. Nearby restaurants include Taco Bell and Campanello's Pizza, while grocery stores such as FreshFoods and Foodsmart are within walking distance. Why not make yourself at home in this quiet and friendly neighborhood?

Rental rates	$1,225/month (Tenant pays all utilities. We bill water and trash to you in addition to rent.)
Qualification Requirements	A deposit (equal to rent) plus one full month's rent must be paid when signing a contract. Minimum 12-month lease. $45 non-refundable application fee.
Additional notes	Renter's insurance required. This is a smoke-free home.
Pets allowed	Dogs, cats (3-pet maximum, $30/month).

To:	inquiries@jonesrealestate.com
From:	pt.godfrey@ridleyarnold.com
Date:	March 13
Subject:	Everglade Drive property

Dear Ms. Jones,

I'm mailing with an inquiry about the Peytonville property advertised on your Web site. Could you kindly clarify some points for me?
1. Your advertisement states that the property is surrounded by green space. Is this space part of the property—or is it a public area?
2. You mention a $45 non-refundable application fee. Is this to be paid before or after any contract is signed?

Many thanks for your consideration,

Charles Godfrey

To:	pt.godfrey@ridleyarnold.com
From:	inquiries@jonesrealestate.com
Date:	March 14
Subject:	Re: Everglade Drive property

Dear Mr. Godfrey,

Thank you for your interest in our Everglade Drive property. Let me answer your questions. The green space that surrounds the property is a public area, not part of the property. Also, the application fee should be paid before any contract is signed.

Please feel free to ask me if you need any more information.

Best regards,

Samantha Jones
Jones Real Estate

9. On the Web page, what is indicated about the property?

(A) Utilities are included in the monthly rent.
(B) There are no grocery stores within walking distance.
(C) Up to two pets are allowed.
(D) Smoking is not allowed.

10. On the Web page, the word "tenant" in paragraph 2, line 1, is closest in meaning to

(A) landlord
(B) renter
(C) property
(D) owner

11. Who most likely is Ms. Jones?

(A) A real-estate agent
(B) A Web designer
(C) An insurance agent
(D) A lawyer

12. What does Mr. Godfrey want to know?

(A) When the deposit should be paid
(B) The amount of the application fee
(C) Whether the green space is part of the property or not
(D) Whether the application fee can be refunded or not

13. How much does Mr. Godfrey need to pay before signing the contract to rent the property?

(A) Nothing
(B) $45
(C) $1,225
(D) $2,450

Communicative Training

Part 7 で取り上げたウェブページを使ってパートナーと英語で互いに質問をしてみましょう。
答える際は、"Yes." や "No." だけで終わらないよう適宜、情報を追加しましょう。

Student A
Student B（パートナー）に下記の質問をしてみましょう。

Student B
Student A（パートナー）の質問に対して Part 7 の英文を見ながら答えましょう。

1. How many bathrooms are there in the Peytonville property?
2. Are there restaurants near the property?
3. How much is the rent?
4. Is the application fee refundable?
5. Can residents keep pets in the property?
6. Is smoking allowed in the property?
7. (You choose!)

本テキストで取り上げている接尾辞一覧

名詞を作る接尾辞

接尾辞	意味		例
-ant	人	～する人	applicant（応募者）（< apply）
-ee		～される人	employee（従業員）（< employ）
-er		～する人	employer（雇用主）（< employ）
-ian		～する人	magician（手品師）（< magic）
-ist		～な人、～する人	specialist（専門家）（< special）
-or		～する人	educator（教育者）（< educate）
-ence	こと、状態		existence（存在）（< exist）
-ion, -sion, -tion			invention（発明）（< invent）
-ity, -ty			security（安全）（< secure）
-ment			excitement（興奮）（< excite）
-ness			politeness（礼儀正しさ）（< polite）
-th			width（広さ）（< wide）

形容詞を作る接尾辞

接尾辞	意味	例
-able	～できる	imaginable（想像できる）（< imagine）
-al	～の	additional（追加の）（< addition）
-ed	～された	satisfied（満足した）（< satisfy）
-ent	～な	excellent（極めて優れた）（< excel）
-ful	～に満ちた	careful（注意深い）（< care）
-ing	～させるような、～している	exciting（興奮させるような）（< excite）
-ive	～な	active（活動的な）（< act）
-less	～のない	careless（不注意な）（< care）
-ory	～な	satisfactory（満足できる）（< satisfy）
-ous	～な	dangerous（危険な）（< danger）

動詞を作る接尾辞

接尾辞	意味	例
-ate*	~にする	originate（始まる）（< origin）
-en		widen（~を広くする）（< wide）
-fy, -ify		simplify（単純化する）（< simple）
-ize		specialize（専門にする）（< special）

＊必ずしも動詞とは限らず、fortunate（幸運な）のように形容詞を作る場合もあるので注意が必要。

副詞を作る接尾辞

接尾辞	意味	例
-ly*	~なように	specially（特別に）（< special）

＊必ずしも副詞とは限らず、weekly（毎週の）のように形容詞を作る場合もあるので注意が必要。

主な接頭辞一覧

接頭辞	意味	例
bi-	2つの（two）	bimonthly（隔月の）（< monthly）
dis-	~でない（not）	dissatisfied（不満な）（< satisfied）
in-, im-, il-, ir- ※ im- は p や m で始まる形容詞、ir- は r で始まる形容詞、il- は l で始まる形容詞の前につくことが多い。	~でない（not）	incomplete（不完全な）（< complete） impossible（不可能な）（< possible） immature（未熟な）（< mature） illegal（不法の）（< legal） irregular（不規則な）（< regular）
mono-	1つの（one）	monorail（モノレール）（< rail）
multi-	多くの（many）	multimillion（数百万の）（< million）
non-	~でない（not）	nonprofit（非営利の）（< profit）
post-	後の（after）	postwar（戦後の）（< war）
pre-	前に（before）	prewar（戦前の）（< war）
re-	再び（again）	restart（再出発する）（< start）
semi-	半分（half）	semiautomatic（半自動の）（< automatic）
un-	~でない（not） 元に戻して（back）	uneasy（不安な）（< easy） undo（元に戻す）（< do）

本テキストで取り上げているつなぎ言葉一覧

意味	つなぎ言葉
結果（したがって、そのため）	as a result（その結果） therefore（それゆえ） thus（したがって）
逆接（しかし、ところが）	however（しかしながら） nevertheless（それにもかかわらず）
情報追加（さらに、しかも）	furthermore（その上） in addition（その上） moreover（さらに）
例示（例えば）	for example（例えば） for instance（例えば）
順序（まず、それから、最後に）	first（最初に） next（次に） then（それから） finally（最後に）
条件（さもなければ）	otherwise（さもなければ）
対比（それに対して）	on the other hand（一方で）

本テキストで取り上げている定型表現一覧

	例文	下線部の意味
イベントの発表、告知	Macy's <u>is pleased to announce</u> the opening of its new store.	～を発表いたします
	Visitors <u>are encouraged to use</u> public transportation.	～をご利用ください
	The concert <u>takes place</u> next Thursday.	開催される
	His latest movie <u>features</u> an all-star cast.	～を呼びものとする
求人案内	Please <u>send your résumé</u> to Kate Ross.	履歴書を送る
	<u>Applicants must have</u> a university degree in tourism.	応募者には～が必要です
	<u>Duties include</u> frequent visits to clients.	職務には～が含まれます
	We are looking for someone <u>with a background in</u> marketing.	～の経歴がある
eメールや手紙	<u>Please find attached</u> the schedule for the seminar.	～を添付いたします
	I <u>look forward to hearing from you</u>.	お返事をいただければ幸いです
	<u>Thank you for your inquiry</u> regarding our products.	お問い合わせありがとうございます
	<u>Thank you in advance</u>.	よろしくお願いいたします
保守点検等の告知	<u>Please be informed</u> that we will be closed on December 25 for Christmas.	～をお知らせします
	Thank you for your <u>patience</u> and cooperation.	ご辛抱
	The programs may change <u>without notice</u>.	予告なしに
	We apologize for any <u>inconvenience</u> this may cause you.	ご迷惑

TEXT PRODUCTION STAFF

edited by	編集
Minako Hagiwara	萩原 美奈子
Takashi Kudo	工藤 隆志

cover design by	表紙デザイン
Nobuyoshi Fujino	藤野 伸芳

illustration by	イラスト
Yoko Sekine	関根 庸子

CD PRODUCTION STAFF

recorded by	吹き込み者
Jack Merluzzi (AmE)	ジャック・マルージ (アメリカ英語)
Rachel Walzer (AmE)	レイチェル・ワルザー (アメリカ英語)
Nadia McKechnie (BrE)	ナディア・マケックニー (イギリス英語)
Stuart O (AsE)	スチュアート・オー (オーストラリア英語)
Neil DeMaere (CnE)	ニール・デマル (カナダ英語)

A COMMUNICATIVE APPROACH TO
THE TOEIC® L&R TEST Book 1: Elementary
コミュニケーションスキルが身に付く
TOEIC® L&R TEST《初級編》

2022年1月20日　初版発行
2024年3月5日　第4刷発行

著　　者　　角山 照彦　　Simon Capper　　遠藤 利昌

発 行 者　　佐野 英一郎

発 行 所　　株式会社 成 美 堂
　　　　　　〒101-0052　東京都千代田区神田小川町3-22
　　　　　　TEL 03-3291-2261　FAX 03-3293-5490
　　　　　　https://www.seibido.co.jp

印 刷・製 本　　三美印刷株式会社

ISBN 978-4-7919-7252-4　　　　　　　　　　　　Printed in Japan